# PERSUASION TECHNIQUES

*MENTAL MODELS AND PSYCHOLOGY OF SELLING ON HOW TO DEAL WITH DIFFICULT PEOPLE AND GET WHAT YOU WANT.*

# Table of Contents

# Introduction

Aristotle's *Rhetoric* identified the foundations of persuasion as ethos, logos, and pathos. Ethos is what determines the credibility of the person doing the persuasion. Logos regards the logic that goes into the persuasion, and pathos is the emotional appeal to the person who is being persuaded.

For example, say you are trying to persuade someone to try out a new diet. You would first make yourself credible by stating that you are a trained physician, or perhaps that you recently lost weight from the same diet. You would then appeal logically by stating facts about the diet, especially ones based on scientific research.

Finally, you would emotionally appeal to the audience by using relatable ideas, such as the struggle to find a swimsuit that fits. These three elements are going to be the most important factors in becoming a person who can persuade others.

Persuasion requires the persuader to look at who they want to persuade and determine what they can do or say to them in order to get their way. As the persuader, you have a goal in mind. You want to get something from the other person. Perhaps you want to persuade your boss to hire your friend. Your goal would be to convince your boss that your friend is the best candidate.

You would specifically pick out what to say to your boss until you have reached your goal. If you went about it over a long period of time, maybe by slowly bringing your friend around to get to know your boss, that tactic would be more related to influence. Persuasion refers to when you are attempting to get someone to fulfill a specific goal.

There are obvious forms of persuasion present all around us. At any given moment, you can walk down the street and see at least one advertisement that is informing you of a great deal. Maybe it is "buy one get one free," "spend more, pay less," or some other claim that is trying to persuade you to give the company your money.

Persuasion isn't always this obvious, but it is important to understand all levels of persuasion so we can better avoid or mimic them. Many of our friends are persuasive. They will say things like "You should go to John's party on Friday" because they don't want to go to the party alone.

We also have to be wary of the way that persuasion can be harmful. When its intention is no longer to mutually benefit both parties, there might be some form of manipulation involved. When you are the one being persuaded, it isn't always easy to identify what is happening. Sometimes you might not realize until it is too late. You might end up going to John's party and realize that it is filled with boring people you don't know, but your friend persuaded you to go because they wanted you there so that they did not get bored.

Persuasion occurs much quicker than influence. You will usually come up with a strategy for the persuasion before as well, where influence might end up happening without even trying. In order to be good at persuasion, it is something that you have to practice. Since sometimes you only have one shot, you have to make sure that you are not going to ruin your chance to be persuasive.

Influence can make it easier to convince someone of something or to recover when you have failed to do it. If you persuade someone to do something and get caught and labeled as a manipulator, it can ruin your credibility. Not all forms of persuasion are bad, but some people are wary that you might be trying to control them, so if done in the wrong way, it can make them turn away from you.

Even a thirty-second ad can be persuasive. There is no time limit that says how quickly or how slowly you can persuade someone. You might have a year to persuade someone to move to a different neighborhood, or you might only have a minute to persuade them to sign a lease for a new apartment.

In either scenario, the right persuader would have no problem trying to convince the other person to do what they want. If something takes too long, however, it might turn into a form of influence, or you might just have to find a different way to be persuasive.

Sometimes you do not even have to say anything; just a look can be enough to persuade. Someone might be trying on a certain outfit, and without saying that it makes them look bad, the look on your face can be enough to make them realize they should choose something different.

At the same time, we also have to look at how not saying anything can persuade someone to make a certain decision. If someone talks about wanting to do something, and you give them a simple head shake, they might be persuaded not to follow through with it at all and pursue something else instead.

Even though it can be short term, moments of persuasion can have long-term effects. If you did persuade someone to sign a lease within a short period of time, that lease could be for twelve months, and that person is now committed to a certain apartment. Before you attempt to persuade, you have to ensure that it is going to be mutually beneficial for both parties.

### *Technique over Relationship*

You do not have to have a close relationship with the person you are persuading. Sometimes we can persuade the sales clerk to give us a discount, or we can persuade a customer to go through with a larger sale. While influence requires a longer-term relationship, persuasion can be accomplished from the moment you meet someone.

You must be a persuasive person in order to carry through the motivation for a choice one way or another. If you come off as untrustworthy, or someone who is not authentic, it is going to be harder to be persuasive. Persuasiveness comes naturally for some, but it can certainly be learned by even the most suspicious-looking people.

Influence occurs with people who might have been admiring the influencer for a while, so it is easier to become influenced by them. Persuasion requires a little more work. You do not have that trust to fall back on, so you have to make sure that you are building an authentic case for yourself.

Give the other person a reason to trust you, and don't let them down. If you do, it will cause them to run.

There are teams hired by different marketers specifically to study persuasive techniques. Some people even do research studies to determine how someone might be easily persuaded.

Also, there are psychologists who specialize in persuasion and influence, so you can start to understand just how powerful this tool can be. It is not about building a relationship with someone. Instead, it is about finding the right technique to make sure that you are persuading properly. Having a relationship helps, but then that will start becoming a method of influence.

Think of a brand that you love that does not really advertise much. There is a good chance they built up a reputation and have been around for decades. People are influenced by their products, so they buy them. Newer companies have to do more to try and persuade you to try out their products than the ones that you already trust.

Many politicians will use persuasive techniques as well. You may not know about political candidates until they start to post their ads on television. In these advertisements, they will do whatever they can to make sure that they are persuading you to believe in them. They use techniques, strategies, and tactics backed by psychologists to persuade you.

Someone you already follow will be more influential, but for the most part, political candidates are trying to persuade you to vote for them. Next election season, look for all the methods of persuasion that people are using.

Most of the sales happen because you hear something or someone buy and generally the word spreads through various medium. Would someone like to buy something that they haven't heard of till now in life? If at all they wish to buy, what could be the possible reasons and then would it be a product or a service. There is a pattern and a system one needs to understand how to sell and close a sale to anybody.

This book unfolds the secrets and tips to sell and close anybody that are time tested and proven. It basically starts with what your customer needs and how often they try to buy a product or a service. You will feel everything is under control, however let us look at certain scenarios that are common –

1.    Whenever someone tells you that it is not enough if you just close a sale, but how to open and maintain a relationship.

2.    At times you may wonder that while you have lots of customers, why to look for new ones.

3.    You have an exclusive business that makes you feel you are the creator.

After reading the book, you will be able to understand the logic behind sales closures, from a salesman's perspective and from a customer's perspective. It is in5tended to be a guide that will serve the purpose of teaching you a thing or two about making the right choices for your products and services and is a guide for both the salesman and the customer. Well, everyone wants more, different and something new to show. For that matter, there is a lot of difference in the way customers perceive and understand buying anything. Simply, you wouldn't like to buy a comb the way you buy a hair gel.

The book identifies every need and scenario a salesman would go through and highlights possible solutions which will be of help in closing a sale. There are tips for everybody and will not concentrate on just one group of people. There is enough information to suit everyone and help them make a choice for themselves. The book is divided into various headings where each one will tell a separate story. It will ultimately help everyone in their pursuit to buy and sell products and services that will prove to be extremely useful.

The book will give you a glimpse of what it takes to both retain a customer and cause him or her to bring in more. Imagine having a number of customers who are all willing to bring in newer ones that are just as interested in buying your product or service. Will that not be good? It will completely turn your business around and you will have a good business. This book will try and tell you the secrets of finding new customers and also increasing your business potential. There are many people who wish to increase their customer base and this is easy to do if you follow the steps and techniques mentioned in this book.

**How many people have you met lately?**

To understand what needs to be sold and how to sell it, it is obvious that you need to get the pulse and what is the flavor of the season. People love to spread word about something that they buy and that word is precious. They will speak about something that has caught their fancy and others will try and copy them just to remain with the trend that is popular for the season.

So as a company looking to improve sales, there can be a million things to consider when you decide to sell a product. You cannot simply assume your customer will like something just by looking at a past trend. You need to understand what will please your customers and what it will take for them to buy your product or service. You cannot sell sweaters in summer and should wait until the rainy season to have your products sold.

Similarly, you need to make sure that people are ready to buy what you offer to them and more importantly, whether your upgraded product will be a hit amongst the existing customers. You must do your market research and for this, you need to take the right steps. You must understand how to persuade customers and convert them into complete buyers. You must take measures to help them make a choice for themselves. You need to tell them how you are bothered about them long after they have made their purchase.

Everything will count when you wish to make new customers and try and retain the old ones. This may consist lot of factors ranging from climatic conditions, buying behavior, economic conditions, trends and above all customer's interest levels which will be the most important criteria to consider as you will have to bear in mind their likes and dislikes to cater to them appropriately. This book covers details pertaining to the ways in which you can understand customer requirements, moods and what information you should seek when you try to gather information related to close your sale.

# Chapter 1 Why is Persuasion Important?

Persuasion is an appeal to an audience. It is the process of influencing an individual's behavior, intentions, beliefs, attitudes, or motivations through communication, without compulsion. When it comes to business, persuasion aims at altering an individual's or a group's behavior or attitude towards another person, an object, an idea, or event. This can be achieved using verbal or written communication to deliver information, express feelings, or demonstrate logic. Persuasion is also a tool used in pursuing personal gain. This is usually evident in election campaigns, trial advocacy, or sales pitch. It can also be interpreted as persuasion when one uses one's position and resources to try to change or influence people's attitudes and behaviors.

Persuasion is the art of convincing someone about something. There is nothing underhand about persuasion, seeing as though one person makes his or her case and lets the other decide whether or not they buy it. The intentions of the persuader are known right from the beginning since they are exactly what they are trying to get the other to believe. It is precisely because of this reason why many people may not consider persuasion as a form of manipulation. They take it to be more of a discussion where the best argument carries the day. However, that is just one side of the coin.

There are a number of ways in which a person may be persuaded to do something. This section will, however, deal with the two main ones. These are; convincing people through logical reasoning, and persuasion by leveraging one's emotions. Before discussing either of the two, it is important to highlight what persuasion may be used to achieve. In many cases, persuasion is used to elicit certain behaviors from people. Mostly, it is used to get people to conform to another's ideas. It may also be used to; convince people to do something they are reluctant to do, to motivate people to do something they are already doing, to stop them from doing what they are doing or what they intend to do, or to cause others to change their beliefs about something and to adopt new ones.

## History of Persuasion

Persuasion commenced with the Greeks. They held elocution and rhetoric as the highest standards for a politician to succeed. At that time, all trials used to be held in the assembly front, with the prosecution and defense, both resting on the speaker's ability to persuade. Rhetoric was, at any instance, the capacity to come up with the persuasion means available. Aristotle, the Greek philosopher, coined four reasons as to why someone should master the science of persuasion as follows:

- It is the best way to defend oneself

- It helps to argue both sides of the problem by understanding it and considering all the options

- It is a speaker's fault when a case in question fails to win, given the perfect nature of truth and justice

- Persuasion is an excellent teaching tool

**Modes of Persuasion**

The speaker's appeal to the audience is classified by the modes of persuasion, which are the devices in rhetoric. They are also called rhetoric appeals or ethical strategies. They are:

- Pathos

- Logos

- Ethos

- Kairos

According to Aristotle's rhetoric, a matter is believed to be well demonstrated, when the audience is fully persuaded. Therefore, demonstration acts as a way of persuasion. Spoken words thus can achieve persuasion in three ways as follows:

- When the speech is presented very well as to make the audience think the speaker believable, then persuasion is arrived at by the presenter's personal character.

- When the speech stirs emotions of the hearers, then persuasion may come through them.

- Persuasion is achieved through the speech itself. This is when an apparent truth or a truth is proved using an argument that is persuasive and which favors the case being discussed.

## Ethos

Ethos is a Greek word that means character. It is used to describe the guiding ideals and beliefs that govern a nation, community, or ideology. The Greeks also used this word to relate to the power of music in influencing behaviors, emotions, or even morals. In rhetoric, ethos appeals to the credibility or authority of the speaker. It refers to the ability of the speaker to convince the audience that he qualifies to speak on the subject. For Aristotle, it was used as a strategy by an orator to inspire trust in the audience. This can be achieved in the following ways:

- Being a notable figure in the area of discussion

- Having mastered the terms associated with the area in question

- when a bona fide from renowned authorities introduces you

## Pathos

Pathos is an appeal to the audience's emotions to elicit feelings. Empathy, sympathy, and pathetic are all derivative terms of pathos. One way to use it is in the form of a passionate delivery, metaphor, or smile. It can also come as a vague claim that a particular action or matter is against the principles of truth and justice. Pathos can become very potent when utilized well, but a speech cannot depend on pathos solely. If a speaker can demonstrate a connection with an underlying value of the audience, then pathos becomes most effective.

A speaker can sway the audience by using pathos and fear. Pathos also involves appeals to the listeners' hopes or imaginations. This is achieved if the orator paints a picture of promising results in the future, after rising to the proposed course of action. Sometimes, a speaker can downplay ethos while putting more emphasize on pathos, to achieve the intended appeal.

 **Logos**

Logos is a Greek word with various meanings such as plea, expectation, ground, opinion, discourse, account, speech, and proportion. The term was used in different ways by ancient Greek Philosophers. The sophist used the word to refer to discourse, while Aristotle used the term to mean to reasoned discourse.

Logos refers to logical appeal or its simulation. It describes figures or facts to anchor the views and ideas of the speaker. Ethos is enhanced by having a logos appeal. This is because logos appeal makes the audience to see the speaker as knowledgeable and well prepared because of the information. However, sometimes, the data can be complicated and confusing and end up confusing the listeners. Also, logos can be inaccurate and misleading, regardless of how relevant to the subject at hand it may seem. Falsified, inaccurate, or is-contextualized data can be used in some cases to enact a pathos effect.

# Kairos

Kairos is a Greek word meaning the critical, the opportune moment, or the right time for action. It is a passing instant when an opportunity appears, and must be driven through with force so that success can be achieved. It was essential to the sophists, who emphasized the speaker's ability to adapt and use it to his advantage, as the contingent circumstances changed. In Aristotle's rhetoric, it is the context of time and space in which proof was to be delivered.

In other words, Kairos refers to the time and the place of the speech. It doesn't stand alone, but stand with other contextual elements such as the audience, which refers to the emotional and psychological makeup of the people receiving the proof; and To Prepon, which is the style with which the orator clothes the proof. Using this to his advantage, an orator can persuade the audience to take immediate action. It is used to pressurize the audience. This is also common in sales and discounts.

## Reasons for Persuasion

*To Convince People to Do Something They Are Reluctant to Do*

This is best explained using an example. Picture a situation where you are driving along a muddy road on an especially rainy day when your vehicle gets stuck in the mud. You try your best to maneuver the vehicle out of the mud, but it just won't budge. The harder you try, the worse the situation gets. The road you are stuck in is not one of the main ones and is, therefore, not very well-traveled by other motorists. Because of this, the chances of getting help by being towed by another truck are next to nil. Luckily, there is a diner up ahead right around the corner. You figure that you can get some help there, so you go. At the diner, you find a group of young men just exiting the establishment. Just what you needed, you figure.

You talk to them about your problem, and they listen. They sympathize but are reluctant to help you push your car out of the mud. They tell you that they would if they could, but they aren't willing to get dirty. The only thing left under these circumstances is to use your persuasion to convince them to help you. The best approach for such a scenario is to make their helping you worth their while. For instance, you may offer each one of them a certain amount of money if they help you. Hear, the money acts as a persuasive tool meant to make them change their minds over something that they were initially reluctant to do.

*Persuasion for Motivation*

If you are a supervisor somewhere and aren't happy at the rate at which the employees under you are getting work done. What would be the best way to make them work harder or faster? You may choose to dangle a carrot for the most hardworking employee or talk to them persuasively to get them to do more work faster. Either way, you will be banking on your persuasion skills for motivation. The same can be used to achieve the opposite. To cause people to slow down on what they are doing. Supposing that your partner is stressed over some upcoming interview and just won't give themselves some break to relax. They spend much time preparing and studying for the same; you worry about them.

Here, you will need to persuade them that resting is in their best interest. You may need to point out some compelling reasons why this is the case. For example, you may tell them that if they show up at the interview looking tired and bent out of shape, they may not land the position they are looking forward to. In such a case, persuasion would be critical in making your partner slow down and relax.

*Persuasion for Conformity*

Conformity is one of the main reasons why people persuade others. A significant amount of all conversations, irrespective of where they happen or what they are about, are persuasions aimed at bringing about conformity. People are always trying to convince others to look at things from their own perspective. Take, for example, politicians. Everything that they say when they address the public is done in an effort to try and make them adopt his view of things. All campaign messages are meant to cause people to conform to the speaker's ideologies and policies. To do this, such messages are packaged in a manner that will be appealing to the audience. This is done in order to improve their receptivity.

For any call for conformity to be successful, it must be backed with facts and reason enough. It is not enough to simply tell someone that your view of things is the right one and theirs is not. If you want to get them to adopt your view, you will have to do a lot better than that. You will need to give them compelling reasons why this is the case. This relies on one form of persuasion of using logic and reason.

As stated, this type of persuasion has extensive use. An important area of its application is in trying to get people to drop some bad habits that they pick up along the way. An example of this is such as in trying to get drug addicts to quit abusing drugs. Whereas persuasion may not be sufficient to cause such people to change, its impact is significant. Here, they will be convinced about why staying sober is a good thing and that they should conform to sobriety. In fact, all support groups to this effect are pegged upon the power of persuasion for conformity. People are encouraged to hang out with others and share their struggles in order to motivate each other.

Using an example of such support groups, alcoholics anonymous, recovering alcoholics are always encouraged to join them so that they may persuade each other to conform to the group's goals and to dedicate themselves to quitting. By listening to the struggles of fellow alcoholics and what they do when they have the urge to drink, you become encouraged to keep on the fight. This means that the attendance of such groups relies upon the persuasion of its members to conform.

*Persuasion in Business*

Every conversation that is meant to convince you to buy something is persuasion. The most persuasive salespeople are often the most successful in what they do. They will give you all the reasons why you need to make a particular purchase until you are convinced that it is the right thing to do. For business persuasion to succeed there has to be some sign of interest from the potential buyer. Otherwise, you cannot persuade someone to buy something that they have absolutely no interest in. The trick for successful salespeople is, therefore, to identify signs of interest from shoppers then move in with their persuasion skills to clear any doubts from their minds.

Take for example, that you are a salesperson at an electronics outlet and that you are salaried on a commission basis. Naturally, you would aim to sell as many electronic gadgets as possible in order to maximize your income. Assume that you spot a buyer who is clearly interested in a particular television set that is on display but is simply unable to make up his mind about buying it. What will you do to make them buy the item?

With the first step of establishing interest being over and done with, you will move on to your second move. This is the one where you try to establish some of the reasons for their doubt. A good salesperson must be able to gently coax such information out of their customers. As an example, let us assume that you establish that your customer has financial concerns about the price of the television set. Knowing this, you will then craft your persuasion skills and ideas so that they are in line with your customer's concerns. For instance, you may try to persuade them by telling them that they have the option of acquiring the item on hire purchase terms, or that a purchase of that brand comes with a free installation package. Whatever you choose to tell them, you must ensure that it is precisely what they want to hear. This is done by aligning your arguments with their concerns.

# Chapter 2 Persuasion Skills

Persuasion is the combination and permutation of a number of key skills that standalone and/ or together inspires trust from the listener. It is important that you learn to use them all if you want to become unbeatable at persuasion. As you will observe each one builds on the other and hence, each one is important in its own right.

## Communication Skills

This is one of the most critical skills if you want to be successful. Without communication skills nothing can be achieved. Every person whom you will find at the top will have mastered the art of communication. If you are unable to communicate your concept with perfect clarity, there is no chance selling it – and hence, there would be no positive action.

Communication is often a much too hyped of a concept. If you had to define it quickly, it is best said that "communication is putting across an idea in the simplest possible terms". Clarity is the core of communication skills. Other "ingredients" of good communication skills are:

### *Conviction*

You should believe what you are saying and it should be clear that you do. The greatest motivators (read that as persuaders) are those who come across as believing what they are saying

100%. The strength of your argument should come from your heart; it should be clear that you are 100% behind what you are saying.

## Accuracy

Would you believe someone whose facts keep getting mixed up? You need to do your homework when you are saying something with the aim to persuade them to do something. Become the devil's advocate and look at the argument from both sides – for and against. Anticipate questions – even if you are giving a speech – and answer them to put your listener at ease.

Put yourself in the other person's shoes and counter the doubts that may arise from your proposition. The more accurate your facts are, the better are your chances to persuade the other person to your point of view.

## Eloquence

Fluency of articulation is another important skill when communicating an idea across. What you want to say should flow out effortlessly. People should like to listen to you because what you say makes sense and hangs well together. Therefore using the right words, right phrases and right expressions is very important.

To ensure that you have mastery over the language you need to work hard at your vocabulary and how you use it. When you start talking, people should like to listen to what you have to say because you can hold the argument together in a most eloquent manner.

## *Humor*

There is nothing more attractive than having the power of making people laugh when you speak. In most cases, the most powerful and attractive humor is that which is addressed to self, but occasionally taking a jibe at the listener can also be endearing. When you laugh at yourself it makes you look vulnerable and part-of-the-crowd and hence, immediately accepted.

It is important to keep in mind that you should NEVER use humor unless you can do this well. Practice saying it aloud in front of your friends and the mirror or videotaping what you plan to say, until you perfect it. If you are among those rare people to whom humor comes effortlessly and intuitively you'd do good to use it as often as possible. For those who need to learn it, use it only when you are 100% sure that you have mastered it.

### Listening Skills

Communication is incomplete without listening skills. No matter how well you put your ideas across, if you do not listen to the response and learn how to act upon it, you will never establish a robust connect with your audience. It is vital that you listen to the cues your audience gives you and swerve your discussion to cover those points.

It is important that you listen more and talk less in most cases, because when people talk, they are most vulnerable. They tell about themselves, what they believe, what drives them, what they would like to do, what they find offensive, what they are happy about – and so on. Listening will give you a hold on your audience and you will know how to direct your discussion to get your audience do what you want.

Listening also does one more thing – it connects you to your audience and builds a rapport. Whose company would you prefer? A person who listens to what you say patiently and attentively or one who never stops talking? People love to talk about themselves; all you have to do is ask open ended questions and listen attentively.

### Leadership Skills

You need to come across as a leader to be taken seriously. Leaders are charismatic speakers, avid motivators and solution finders among others. Charisma is often thought to be a trait that you are born with. Not true; it is just mastering the art of connecting with people.

Charismatic people instill trust and attract followers – and this happens when you feel confident about yourself and what you are doing. Confidence is something that puts you in the lead wherever you go. They say that you'd recognize a king or a queen in a crowd no matter how they are dressed because of the way they carry themselves. They move like they are in total control of the world; and that is something that is exceptionally inspiring.

Timid people, people with low self-esteem would not be able to persuade anyone because of their lack of self-assurance. It is impossible to want to listen or be convinced by one who is not sure of himself.

## Problem Solving Skills

There are only two kinds of people in this world whom you will never forget, the problem solver and the problem maker. Who do you want to be? Obviously, you would rather be the problem solver. People tend to respect those who have ability to look beyond a crisis and find solutions. People like to be around such people because it makes them feel safe.

How do you develop problem solving skills? It is not easy, of course. However, contrary to common belief, it is not too difficult either. Next time you are facing any type of crisis on a personal or professional level try these steps:

- Remove yourself from the immediate crisis and calm your mind. You may use meditation, deep breathing exercises, or simply take a long walk.

- Resist the temptation to find someone to pin the blame, even if that someone could be you. Do not bother with the why at this time.

- Look at what-next step. What needs to be done immediately to minimize the harm and prevent further damage? What is the first step that needs to be done?

- Take action. Take action now. Put one step in front of the other if you cannot see too far in what needs to be done. If you start taking action, you would find that one thing leads to another and suddenly you would stumble upon the solution. People however, will remember and appreciate you for the strength that you showed when you took that first step of action.

### Learning-On-Your-Feet Skills

You will often land in the midst of people who speak a total different language (belong to a different school of thought). They could be from a different world, different culture, and different outlook and hence, try your best, you could not connect with them on the premises you have ready for persuasion. In such cases, you need to learn on your feet.

You need to use your observation and communication skills to understand what they want and what they don't and guide your dialogue accordingly. Learning-on-your-feet is a skill that will come in handy anywhere you go, but it is especially useful when you are trying to persuade anyone and find that they do not share your bandwidth.

## Observations Skills

Observation skill is the very foundation of leadership and communication. You need to master the art to read a person within the first one minute of meeting him. With larger a audience, you need to do your homework well plus feel their pulse when you talk so you can improvise accordingly.

The way a person dresses, is groomed, talks, stands/ sits, holds his head, etc. tell you something about the person. Sharpen these skills by practicing, practicing and practicing. A person with great observation powers will suffer from no set back because they would be relying upon their astute observation powers to learn about their audience. Observation skills are like having a dossier on the person you are talking to; hence, you know what to say and when so you could get him do what you want.

## Motivation Skills

The ability to motivate people is very important. Motivation is however, a little different from persuasion. When you motivate someone, you need to connect the person to the 5 needs, i.e. esteem needs, social needs, safety needs, and psychological needs. Persuasion on the other hand focuses on a 6th need, i.e. YOUR needs.

Persuasion requires that you include and find a connection between your needs and your audience needs. Motivation skills are important because these teach you how to identify personal needs of your audience and by doing so, how to link it with your purpose.

### Selling Skills

Selling skills are among the most important foundation skills for persuasion. Selling includes almost all the skills we spoke about earlier:

### *Education or Awareness*

Selling requires that your audience is educated on the merits of the proposal vis-à-vis their own needs and setting.

### *Collaboration*

It also requires that there is a basic platform for collaboration between you and your audience where both benefit. Persuasion means you get the person do something you want him to do, but also which is beneficial to him.

### *Listening*

You cannot sell without learning to listen. Listening will tell you what is important to your audience and gives you a foot-in-the-door towards your goal.

### *Understanding*

Understanding has two meanings here, i.e. understanding what your audience wants and building on it; and understanding how to use a certain situation to your advantage so you can persuade your target to do as you want them.

*Helping*

Selling means helping your audience to do something better, easier, faster – you bring in a change that is beneficial to their life in some manner.

*Finding Solutions*

Selling almost always offers a solution to a problem or difficulty. The better your ability to highlight the problem and your solution, the quicker you have the target accept your solution; the quicker you can persuade them to do what you want.

*Connecting*

An integral part of selling is building trust, a rapport where the other person believes that you have his best interest as heart. Without connecting with the person at core levels, you cannot achieve much.

*Achieving Goals*

Selling is showing the target the larger picture. Say, you are selling medicine; you will connect it to the goal every person has to stay healthy and pain free. Your methods need to build and highlight the roadmap to achieving these goals to be persuasive.

**Marketing Skills**

Marketing and selling are often mentioned in the same breath and used interchangeably. However, they are different. While selling is micro level, marketing is macro level. Selling focuses on a certain aspect; marketing focuses on the environment, on the overall ambiance. Among top marketing skills are:

## Storytelling

Marketing is all about creating a great story where your target audience gets involved emotionally. Marketing is grabbing attention and holding it until you pull in your audience into the context of your story.

## Testing Waters

Marketing is also about testing perceptions, beliefs, moods, feelings and trends among others. Knowing what you can push and how much you can push and when you can push comes from market testing. If your premise goes against your target's beliefs or feelings, it would be difficult if not impossible to persuade them to go your way.

## Build On Past Experiences

Your persuasion powers will grow with experience. A key marketing skill is to build upon past experiences, continuously analyzing the successes and failures of past endeavors.

## Deliverables

While deliverables are counted as integral part in every endeavor, it is especially important in marketing as it provides indicators and milestones that measure progress. This not only gives you a direction, but also keeps you motivated to plough ahead and achieve your goals.

# Chapter 3 Fundamental Skills For Successful Sales

## It all starts with the basic desire

In order to capture the basic desire of what someone wants is derived by having a marketing strategy in place to identify and sell a product or service. The best strategy is often knitted around the resources that are available with you. Depending on whether you have a lot of less, you need to go as per your budget. If you have only a few resources to employ, you will have to plan it out strategically and decide on what can be employed and where.

It is essential that you remain as intelligent and alert as possible and cut down on unnecessary wastage of precious resources. If you have a lot of resources at your disposal, you will still need to plan it out as it is essential for you to make the most of what you have. Some people go about it without a basic plan and end up wasting whatever is available to them. You will have to first take stock of everything that you have and then decide on what you will use and what you can save for later. You will need resources to conduct market research on the type of audience that is fit for your product and also the target customers.

You also need it for the research and development of the product that you wish to customize for your audience. All in all, you must be prepared with the right plan and the correct amount of resources to help you zero in on a product or service that will help make it easy for you to sell and for the customer to buy.

Imagine if you identified that your market needs high end flashy stuff with premium and elite tags and if you have the resources you may think of getting into it in a flash of a second. But if you don't have the resources you may wait or borrow to make it happen. Both cases you may end up in a risk of cash trapped situations if you have not understood the game properly. So the key is to follow a course of action that is befitting of a customer's wants. You will only be as good as your resource utilization. So try and make the best of the money, men and material resources that you have and use it to help you in your mission to understand and cater to the right type of audience.

**So what do you do?**

You should identify a market strategy that revolves around the buying habits of your customers and what you are planning to sell them. It is easily understood that there is a difference between selling a pen and selling a house. You need to understand the various situations and more importantly the details of the product or service that you are trying to sell.

You need to put yourself in place of the customer and analyze the situation. There should be no doubts in your mind in terms of who to sell it to. Everything should be clearly laid down and you must know who will take a fancy to what. Once you have sold your product to a particular customer, he or she will become your target again. This is because when you first buy, your reasoning as a customer is totally different from the next time you buy.

So, like it's said earlier in this book, that it is much easier to sell it to an existing customer than to sell it to someone totally new. If you have managed to get someone to come and buy your product then it is also possible for you to get them to buy more. This is easier than running after others who may or may not show an interest in what you are selling to them. It is not just easy but also a safe option as you can be rest assured of having a certain number of people coming back to you for their product and service needs.

Do some more research on your existing customers and find out what made them buy and the different situations that made them buy. Find out if you were good at doing something that attracted them in the first place and if that same tactic can be used again to make your customers stay.  Remember that a happy person is like to shop with lots of excitement and chooses anything with lots of cheers and positivity. And if someone is unhappy the outcome is expected that they usually shop in a very dejected way. And an intelligent customer always tries to shop with logic and applies lots of math, calculations and reasoning.

So you need to do a thorough research on whether or not you are able to use something on someone again and make them remain loyal to your products or service. Finally, you need to make sure you also try and find new customers but not make it a top priority. Your top priority should be your current customers alone and attracting new customers can be your second priority.

# Chapter 4 Principles and Tools of Persuasion

The psychology of persuasion is based on six principles, namely:

- Scarcity

- Reciprocity

- Sympathy and like-ability

- Authority

- Commitment and consistency

- Social proof

**Reciprocity**

We are compelled by social norms to react to favor and respond with another favor. We do that naturally so that we do not seem as being ungrateful. It is much easier to have someone do something for you after giving them a gift or doing something for them. This generates makes them feel obligated, and such a feeling of obligation inclines them to consent to your request.

Initiating a favor can result in so many reciprocations of the favor in the future. This principle is widely applied in sales and marketing, where free samples and giveaways are used to initiate transactions. When using the principle of reciprocity to influence others, it is good to be careful. First, you should have a clear understanding of your target audience, what they want, and why you want to influence them.

## Consistency and Commitment

There is a tendency in every human being to want to appear consistent before others. There is an inherent need in us to be consistent with want we have bought, what we said and what we've done. We feel the pressure to act following our prior commitments when making new decisions. For example, you can keep old customers with ease that you can attract new ones.

Commitment is fueled by the desire to appear or look like someone consistent in behavior and attitudes over time. We are more likely to consistently go through a plan after we commit to it publicly. For example, let us say that you have five restaurants where you can call to order a meal. You call three of them to order supper, for three different types of food. By the time you pass by each restaurant to collect your foods, you find that only one restaurant has prepared the food well and it is ready, but for others, you will have to wait for thirty more minutes. The chances are high that next time when you need the same service, you will not call the two restaurants where you were delayed for thirty minutes. You will feel compelled to call the one that served you well because you think that they will be consistent in their commitment to serve you well.

## Social Proof

When we are faced with uncertainty, and we really don't know which decision to make, we observe what others are doing for some social proof or evidence of whether something is good or not.

For example, let us say that you arrive in a new city unfamiliar to you. You go looking for a restaurant, and you come across two restaurants that look quite similar. One is empty, and the other one is almost full. Which one will you choose?

At that moment, you will rely on what others are doing to make your decision, and you will find yourself choosing the almost full restaurant. To be accepted by our society or social sub-groups, we tend to act in the same way as our community does, even if it is wrong. Also, if you know the truth, you may find yourself doing wrong with the masses, other than turning around and telling them the truth. We tend to follow trends, and marketers have mastered the art harnessing the power of social proof.

## Sympathy/ Like-ability

The chances are high that we can get influenced by the people we like. If someone you love wants or asks you to do something, you are more likely to do it. Even something superficial as the physical appearance of someone can influence you to do something for them. When you like someone, you want to reflect on them. If the people you like are doing something, you also want to be part of doing it because you want to be associated with them. You will be influenced by ease to support a cause that your family, colleague, and friends also support so that you can find safety in them by reflecting what they are doing and doing it as well. Companies use this principle with great success when they send sale agents in their communities. It is more likely that people will buy from others who are like themselves, people they know and respect or friends. Sympathy is, therefore, key to influencing buyers. People will rarely buy something from someone they don't like.

When you reflect someone else's behavior, such as dressing in a way that aligns with their interests, speaking the same language, or copying their body language, they will like you and sympathize with you.

## Authority

People tend to believe people with authority or someone they trust and respect. The ordinary individual will tend to accept what is being said by any individual showing authority without questioning it. A figure of authority can be a politician, a celebrity, or any other local hero, well known to the people. You can influence people in a great way by using a figure of authority to deliver your message, other than having to do it yourself.

In general, people tend to obey authority figures, regardless of whether those authority figures are questionable. It is human nature. That is why companies use persons with authority to advertise their goods. The opinion of such professionals and experts is critical and acts as a testimony to guide customers who are not sure about a purchase.

## Scarcity

People want something more when they realize that its supply is inadequate. When there is a perception that something is limited, it is the nature of human beings to want it more. To buy something when it is the very last one, or in a situation where a perception has been created that the special expires soon is a common human behavior. Businesses use such techniques to make huge sales within a short time. When customers or supporters get some wind that there is limited stock, tickets to an upcoming event being limited, or just a few volunteer positions remaining to be filled, they get a feeling that they might miss out and act quickly to secure their items or positions.

## Elements of persuasion

The first element of this theme is that persuasion is often symbolic. What this means is that persuasion utilizes words, sound as well as images so as to get the message across to the specific victim. The logic behind this is quite simple really. For one individual to be able to persuade another into acting in a particular way, they will need to show them why they should act in said way and not vice versa.

The second key is that persuasion will be used deliberately to affect how others act or think. This one is quite obvious; you don't use persuasion to get them to change if you don't deliberately try to affect others. In order to get the topic to believe the same way they do, the persuader will attempt distinct strategies. This could be as easy as having a discussion with them or presenting proof supporting their point of perspective. On the other hand, to change the mind of the subject, it could involve much more and include more deceptive forms.

The distinctive thing about persuasion is that it enables some type of free will for the topic. In this way, the topic is permitted to create its own decision. For the most part, they don't have to go for it, no matter how hard somebody tries to persuade them of something. The subject might hear about the best car to buy a thousand commercials, but if they don't like that brand or don't need a new vehicle at that time, they won't go out and buy it.

Examples of persuasion can be found everywhere, including when you talk to individuals you know, on the Internet, on radio and television. It is also feasible to deliver persuasive messages by nonverbal and verbal means; although when verbal methods are used it is much more efficient

The ability to influence someone during a conversation and make a decision is necessary in order to become one of the most important people in the world today. This ability is useful in business negotiations, and in everyday life.

In general, the impact on people is not so obvious. The basic idea is that people's behavior is often guided by their subconscious simple desires. And to achieve your goals, you need to understand the simple desires of people, and then make your interlocutor passionately wish for something.

It should be noted that in order to influence people you should NOT try to impose or force them to make a hasty decision. It may seem incredible, but the person that wants to reach a mutually beneficial cooperation becomes a huge advantage compared to those that are trying to impose something on others. If you are willing to put yourself in the shoes of another person from whom you want to get something and understand his/her thoughts, then you do not have to worry about your relationship with the person.

The secret lies in the ability to help the self-affirmation of the interlocutor. It is necessary to make sure that your companion looks decent in his own eyes. First things first, there are six basic principles that will absolutely affect any of your interlocutors.

To achieve their goals, people often use the influence of psychology, which helps to manipulate man. Even in ancient times it can be seen that priests ruled the people, instilling in them that religion is harsh, and everyone will be punished if they cannot follow the established rules and practices. Psychological influence strongly acts on the subconscious, causing the victim being influenced to be led by a skilled manipulator.

If you want to succeed and learn how to manage people, these words of the great American entrepreneur should be your credo. You will grow your personality only when you are in close cooperation with the community. From childhood we develop the basic patterns of behavior and outlook, produced by the long historical, biological and mental development of humankind.

In order to have influence and control over another person, it is required that you know their personality and behavioral traits. Most importantly, learn how to use this knowledge to master the specific methods and techniques of influence and control the behavior of the other, on the basis of his outlook, character, personality type and other important psychological features.

If you want to learn how to manage people, secret techniques in this article will let you know not only the theoretical aspect of the question but also allow the use of this knowledge in real life.

To help people to look beyond the limits of consciousness, professionals use a variety of methods and techniques. One of the most effective of these is hypnosis. This method of direct influence on the psyche, whose essence consists of the introduction of human narrowed state of consciousness, makes it is easy to control someone else's suggestion and management.

Persuasion may involve the use of powerful symbolic words such as freedom, justice, and equality, nonverbal visual signs such as the holy cross, and the flag, and familiar images. Symbols are the tools of the persuader to drive the attitudes and mold opinions.

Although persuasion involves a conscious attempt to influence the person in question, there is a thin line separating it from manipulation. In fact, a persuader may never succeed in the first place if the persuadee denies to give in to the ideas proposed by the persuader. The persuader just provides the arguments for communication and proposes a particular idea.

One thing that remains true in both cases is that persuasion will not just form attitudes but will bring about a change. It involves molding and the reinforcement of attitudes, change of perspectives, and shaping up of new habits.

Persuasion rather requires a free choice to work. The persuader must induce and implant the message conveyed in a manner without being forceful or aggressive; that the persuadee starts thinking in a similar fashion. Then only the persuasion lasts for long. To sum up, persuasion is not about forcing someone to do what you want them to do but making them want what you want them to do.

# Chapter 5 Persuasion in Sales and Marketing

Persuasion is a very important aspect of a business. It is, in fact, the basis of any business and therefore anyone who wants to go into any kind of business must be it online or a stall or own a company generally should learn all the rudiments of communicative persuasion.

Persuasion as a concept is evident in every form of communication and that is why it was stated earlier in this discourse that everyone at a point in their lives must have made use of persuasion. To drive effective business communication, persuasion is needed. Without properly understanding how to use persuasion, the business owner might fall short of customers and find it hard to win people over to his ideas. Here's a list of those that might need to use persuasion in business.

The owner of a small or big business trying to get a customer:

- A person or a company trying to get a contract

- A staff who wants to win a sales pitch

- An employee

- A company who is into media and wants to advertise a product to specific people

- Finally, a customer.

The final party on the list of who will want to use persuasion in business here might come as a bit of a surprise but there are bargains in every business and so during the course of any bargain, the customer also tries the convenience the seller that the price should be brought down to the convenience of both parties.

The question now is how to persuade a person to agree with a person in the business.

Understand your audience: The audience is not necessarily large of people; it could also be a single person or a group of people. One of the most crucial parts of any type of communication is knowing the audience and understanding them. This same criticality is also evident in business persuasion. Those who own a business must be very wary of those who they are passing information to whether an individual or a group of individuals. You have to know what they expect, what they want and what the outcome will be for what is intended. In a nutshell, you need to know what their objective is for the business.

An example is when an employee that wants to go for a conference and is looking to take permission from a boss might only be interested in the issue of the budget. The employee can make the boss see reasons why information from that conference will be beneficial for the conference but first, the employee will have to analyse the bosses' interest to help the employee better his communication with the right persuasive messages.

Another example is when a businessman is looking to sell a product, you should know exactly why your customer will like to buy your product and how it will be beneficial to your customer. By making these findings, the approach will be easier, and this will bring us to the next step.

Choosing the right medium: After knowing your audience and seeing what their interest is, it is also very important to analyse what medium of communication they would prefer. Trying to tell a boss about your absence from work over the phone will not be a good idea. The way people want to get messages really differ and some customers are prone to being convinced to get things in different ways. There is a saying that one should never quit a job over the phone. This is true because it is the wrong medium of communication based on the situation.

An example is when you want to stop to meet with a colleague unexpectedly to discuss a very vital issue. It is only agreeable if the colleague is fine by it. If not, then an email should be first put forward or preferably a call based on what the other colleague wants. In essence, for proper persuasive communication, it is vital to make use of a medium that is very appropriate both to the message being passed and to audiences' preference.

Taking time to listen: Passing information is not a way thing. When communicating to yourself, you are only telling yourself what it is that you already know. When trying to persuade another party, it is very advisable that one pays close attention to what the person is also saying. This way, you will understand that a person's emotional state and also have the power to make use of it to get what you want.

In most types of communication, it is usually a two-way thing, and this is the most effective way to persuade your audience. Often, communicators are so focused on what they want that they fail to understand the point of view or the emotional state of the audience. They do not take time to listen. As much as trying to speak is important in persuasion, listening is also important. This can help one understand the audiences' desires, motivation, interest and concerns. What we have tried to explain here is that as much as you would like to get your communication goal, it is also very important to sit back and listen to your audience.

Building a strong relationship: Having good communication is also bent towards a strong relationship. You cannot persuade a boss without having a good relationship with the boss.

You cannot persuade an audience or a customer without first building a good relationship. It is on the foundation of a good relationship that both the business owner and the customer or a colleague and another colleague can get to communicate better. Through strong relationships, regularity is ensured in business. With whoever we have built a solid and strong relationship with, we can share even our most sensitive issues. We can pass information and get feedback from them. Taking time to groom and build connections even before trying to persuade will make a significant difference in your success with persuading. An example is when an employee is trying to get persuade a boss but has a record of always coming late to work or lateness in the submission of jobs. It's easy to guess that the boss will likely not accept the proposal. This is because the employee has not left himself a good impression or building a good reputation with the boss.

Having known what to do when one wants to persuade, it is very important to state that for entrepreneurs, persuasion is a tool that is used to help get new clients, get a good worker and general move the business to a better level. People who know how to persuade are influential and people like then. They are usually the quiet ones in the room. They speak less and they eventually do, they make sense and are able to make people do things. They also make sure to put the needs of others above theirs. Here are habits of a good persuasive businessperson.

Curiosity and listening: As stated in how to persuade people in a business, one should have the habit to listen to effectively persuade another person. You would need to know what others want on both an emotional and also on a physical level. You should make sure to ask good questions and also listen when the person is speaking. You should be open-ended and begin discussions of this sort. You should demonstrate a genuine interest in what others do. If you can understand others by listening, persuasion will come easy. When you want to know and you are attentive, you have automatically sent a message that you value the person. With time, a reputation of trustworthiness will grow, and this is a great quality will grow.

Honesty: Honesty is normally a quality that s required in any business to for that business to be successful. In essence, for a business to thrive, it has to have its benchmark on transparency. This also goes for anyone who is looking to persuade in business. Your credibility and ability to persuade is dependent on your being able to be very honest in all situations. Dishonesty is very destructive and is capable of misleading others. An intentional lie can ruin your professional reputation. It is true that the truth might sometimes hurt but it is better, to be honest than to lose peoples trust due to dishonesty.

Confidence: Be it a customer, a client or a colleague, you should learn to be confident. The place of confidence cannot be side-lined in business. You should know how to show that you really believe in your ideas and in your proposal. You should also be confident in what you are selling.

Being confident when showing a product will convince a potential customer that what you have to offer is truly effective. To avoid anxiety or even self-doubt, you should remain calm when presenting anything. Also, straightforwardness should be used, do not dabble about the whole thing. State your position and validate it with clear factual points.

Effective voicing: Once you have said something, people will begin to make decisions based on the way you have communicated with them. You do not need to be scared or begin to murmur. When communicating, it is advisable to speak slowly and also know when you're speaking slowly so that you can raise your voice to speak loudly but still clearly.  Making use of brief pauses will make being clear easier. Emphasize your points better and avoid fillers like uh.

Tell a story: People will enjoy your speech better when you are able to chip in a story. A well-told story should be enjoyable ad be themed towards what you have to offer. Stories have the ability to persuade others in the business. It is always good to move away from the stress of business to tell a good story. As opposed to facts, the way people pay attention differs. Your story must be able to make a connection between what the client is thinking and what they are already thinking, what the client believes and what you intend him to believe.

## 10 Characteristics Of Highly Successful Salespeople – Do You Have Any Of Those?

Selling cannot take place on its own. It always needs a salesperson that would make it a good or a bad sale. Effective and successful salespersons aren't trained in a day. They hone their skills out of experience and their innate study of customers' tendencies. Here are 10 characteristics that would make you a winning salesperson. Find out how many of these you possess.

### #1 Determined

A great deal of persistence and determination is needed to be a good salesperson. There would be plenty of instances where you might have to face severe criticism or rejection. During such times, only determination will keep you afloat.

It is not easy to convince someone to buy anything even if it just costs a few dollars. It certainly takes a persevering mindset.

If you want to be a high achiever, don't just give up easily. A good sales person will not just take no for an answer and will be amazing at ensuring that at the end of the negotiations, the customer is convinced that they need to have what is for sale.

### #2 Goal Setters

Nothing works without an aim or goal. Expert salespersons devise short as well as long term goals to meet success. They have clarity over what they want and work strategically towards it. They remain focused towards their goals and work against time to meet them. Ask any good salesperson to show his professional planner and you would see each hour of the day and every day of the week being preplanned to meet certain targets.

Each time you are talking with a prospective buyer, you should have a goal in mind, as this will even give you the motivation to convince the buyer that they need to buy what you are selling.

### #3 Inquisitive

A good salesperson always has questions running through their minds. They remain aware and ask prospective customers intelligent questions. They ask questions to know more about the customer's needs so that they can know how their products and services come into the picture. They are also smart enough to endorse their products through their inquisitiveness.

## #4 Good listeners

Successful salespersons are good listeners. They don't believe in using their own gab to sell their products. Rather, they gently persuade their customers to speak about their needs and then present their products or services in the same light. They first listen carefully and then summarize their selling stance.

If you want customers to buy from you, you need to listen to them so that you can know what their needs are and thus be better placed to show the customer how your product comes into place.

I would personally not want to buy anything from someone who just bombards me with the different benefits of a particular product or service without knowing whether I am interested in those benefits in the first place.

## #5 Passionate

Being passionate is crucial if you want to be a successful salesperson. You have to be passionate about the product or else your selling will remain hollow and bleak. Good salespersons remain ever in love with their products and this increases their chances of selling effectively. Their every argument will be convincing enough and will exude their passion.

## #6 Go-Getters

Successful salespersons cannot afford to be laid back otherwise; they would miss the leads and lose their contacts. They have to be always in close contact with potential buyers' base even on a personal level. Apart from the sales pitch, they remain in touch with the customers to find out how the products they bought are functioning as they should or they are experiencing any challenges. They follow up to know if the services the customer bought are suitable or not. They even call customers to know if they require certain products and services that they may have bought a while back.

A good salesperson will not sit and wait for the customer to ask about a particular product but will send reminders as well as more information about current products and services as well as new product and services being launched so that the customer can know what to expect.

### #7 Confident

If you want to be the best salesperson, you have to be confident, persuasive and self-assured as rejection is a common feature here. Successful salespeople must not lose their heart after hearing a 'no'. Rather, they should be able to convert 'no', 'if' or 'but' into the affirmative like the true challengers they are.

### #8 Patient

Successful salespersons do not rush into any deal, as they know how suicidal that can be. They handle their customers patiently and do not throttle them with their non-stop chatter.

Impatient salespersons would not do justice to their profile for they would not be able to feel the pulse of the market and their customers.

## #9 Adaptable

Successful salespersons are flexible and adaptive to deal with all kinds of situations and customers. If nothing is working, they quickly alter their strategy and shift the pivot. The trick is to sell whatever you are selling in a language that the prospective customer understands.

## #10 Show Empathy

Empathy is simply the ability to identify with customers to feel what they may be feeling and thus make them feel respected. You need to empathize with a customer and the challenges that they may be facing; hence, their need for your product. Once you can identify what they may be feeling, it is very easy to put your product or service in a way that the customer can buy such a product.

Additionally, a salesperson that is able to empathize with customers is likely to gain trust and build rapport with customers, which is crucial if you want to always be making a sale.

# Chapter 6 Using Body Language to Promote Sales

In this chapter, we are going to be taking a closer look at some advanced body language tips. These concepts will help you take your understanding of human nature even further. In addition, you will be able to get a better grasp of your own body language so that you can truly become a master communicator.

When looking into advanced body language, there are tiny movements and cues that can lead you to figure out where a person is both physically and emotionally.

As such, let's take a look at some of these clues. By the end of this chapter, I am sure you will become far more self-conscious of the way you handle yourself especially in meetings and other social interactions.

Now, the first tip we are going to discuss is fidgeting. Fidgeting can be seen in many ways. The most common type of fidgeting in the inability to sit still. Excessive movement can be due to any number of reasons. These reasons range from a person being nervous or uncomfortable to simply being hyperactive and unable to stay in one spot.

Barring some physiological condtion in which a person is simply unable to sit still, fidgeting is most commonly associated with being nervous. Anxiety is generally the root cause of this behavior. So, it is up to you to determine the context in which you find yourself in. That way, you can figure out if the fidgeting is directly related to subject matter being discussed in a meeting or due to the events that are taking place.

Another common cause for fidgeting is boredom. Any teacher will tell you that bored and uninterested students will almost always start fidgeting in their places. In many cases, teachers struggle with students who can't sit still. That only compounds the problem because the student was bored to begin with. Then, the with the teacher's reprimanding, the problem only gets worse.

In a business setting, fidgeting is commonly seen in the clicking of pens, doodling in notebooks or tapping of feet. Aside from boredom, fidgeting behavior can be taken as a flight response. The individual is looking to get away from the situation but may be unable to do so. Hence, they feel trapped. That is why the easiest coping mechanism is fidgeting.

When a person feels trapped in a meeting for example, foot tapping becomes a common reaction. After all, anyone who is constantly moving their feet is looking to get going. The same goes for legs. Excessive leg movement is a sign that the individual is looking to get moving. However, involuntary leg movement does happen as a biological response from the brain when it senses that the individual is falling asleep. This reaction keeps the body awake especially when an individual has not gotten enough sleep.

Similarly, faster than usual blinking can be a sign that a person is getting ready to fall asleep. The reasoning behind faster than usual blinking is that the brain is desperately trying to keep the body from shutting down. Of course, there is a point where the brain is unable to keep the body awake and a person simply dozes off. In extreme cases of sleep deprivation, a person will collapse to the floor and literally go into a coma.

Extreme cases aside, the fact that a person may be fidgeting excessively has more to do with their reaction to what's happening around them then a biological reaction to sleep deprivation. So, pay close attention, if you can, to a person's legs and feet. They will tell you if they are getting ready to hightail it out.

With regard to hands, one of the hallmarks of effective communicators is using hand when speaking. What this does is that it provides a means of emphasizing what they are saying. Also, it gives off the impression that the person is being since about what they are saying.

Any hand gestures that have an open palm can be taken as a positive sign. Unless someone is banding a table with the palm of their hand, you can infer that an open palm is inviting and friendly. Any gesture with a closed hand or fist is almost always seen as a negative sign.

In sports, fist pumping is seen as a sign of victory and power. Naturally, opponents won't appreciate such gestures very much.

Any time you are looking to convey positive feelings, avoid using any closed hand gestures. They will send mixed signals to your audience as they will believe you are being aggressive or forceful.

When sitting, if a person has the palms of their hands on the table, that is palms facing down, you can be sure they are in a closed position. They may be listening to what you have to say, but you will not be able to convince them of your message.

Similarly, a closed hand is definite indicator that your interlocutor is reluctant to hear what you have to say. If you see these types of hand gestures in addition to direct eye contact or even some teeth on display, then you had better get ready for a fight.

If you find palms down but evasive eye contract and/or tight lips, then you might have someone who is reluctant to hear what you have to say because they feel intimidated or concerned about something. This could be an advantageous position for you especially if you are in competition with the other party.

When a person is sitting with their hands facing upward, like when they are holding a pen while taking notes, you have an unconscious sign of openness and acceptance. This will enable you to get your message across more freely. If you are negotiating with clients or suppliers, this hand gesture will provide you with the signal that your counterparts are receptive to your message.

If this gesture is couple with direct eye contact and higher than usual eyebrows, you could be well on your way to closing the deal that you are aiming for. Please bear in mind that any time a person is not sitting with their legs or arms crossed, you are already ahead.

As we have indicated earlier, crossed arms and legs are defensive positions. They indicate that the individual is not open to communicate and is not receptive to incoming communication. That is why many profile photos of professionals send mixed signals.

On the one hand, you have a smiling well-groomed professional usually dressed in a proper suit. Yet, they have their arms crossed across their chest. This type of position is intended to show that they are friendly yet competent and serious. However, at an instinctive really, they seem unapproachable. As such, the smiling face seems almost menacing as if to say, "give it your best shot".

The best profile photos for professionals and business leaders usually depict the individual with their arms open, perhaps holding something, or sitting at their desk with their hands facing upward on the desk. In order to avoid having their hands look strange, they may have an open book and a pen in one hand. Another great accessory is a watch. While the watch itself is meaningless, it just provides symmetry to the image.

Most of the profile pics you see of business leaders feature a headshot of them smiling and looking directly at the camera. Professional profile pics that seem like the individual was caught unaware are uninspiring and do not transmit and friendly and open nature. In fact, it makes it seem like you haven't taken the time to come up with a proper-looking profile photo.

When standing, it is imperative that you avoid putting your hands in your pockets. These is a sign of disrespect in some cultures and will almost always send the wrong message in American culture. If you are giving a presentation, you can hold a marker or clicker in your hands, chest high.

Also, placing your hands behind your back is an instinctive sign that you are hiding something. This may lead you to lose credibility with your audience as they might believe you are not being totally honest them.

If you are up on a stage, pacing back and forth is distracting and almost always leads to people paying more attention to your movements that to your message. It's best to pick one spot and stay there. That way, you won't have to worry about distracting your audience from what you have to say.

On the subject of public speaking, it is always a good idea to avoid turning your back to your audience. While in some cultures it is a total lack of respect to turn your back on someone, it is also a sign of appreciation to always face your audience. If you are writing on a board, you can turn sideways. It might take a bit of practice, but it will pay off as you avoid taking your eyes off your audience.

One helpful tip is to have a podium. With a podium, you can have your notes and you avoid having to move around. Also, the positioning of your hands is not evident. Although, it is a good idea to avoid holding on the sides of the podium for too long. That indicates that you are not entirely relaxed. A good comfortable position at a podium is always highlighted by good posture, head up straight and face looking forward.

Other involuntary mannerism such as adjusting your glasses, playing with your hair, or touching your face are all signs that you are either nervous or uncomfortable. Additionally, it is a great idea to video tape yourself giving a speech as a part of a dry run beforehand. This will allow you to focus on any involuntary mannerism that your audience might find distracting and/or offensive.

On a personal level, it is always a good idea to keep movements to a minimum when speaking to someone. For instance, avoid having things in your hands, such as pens, keys or even your cellphone. That way, your hands won't become a distraction.

Also, gestures such as adjusting your glasses too much or playing with your hand don't always reflect a comfortable attitude. While you don't want to seem like an automaton, you do want to make your movements as natural as they can possibly be. That way you can transmit a feeling of interest and engagement when speaking with someone else.

On the subject of phones, it is best to stay away from them altogether. If you are in a formal business meeting, it is a good idea to just put it away. Any fidgeting with a phone may lead the other party to feel that you are not interested in the meeting. While this point does not necessarily relate to body language or analyzing people, it's just good sense to avoid having phones around.

In personal settings, having a phone on the table is enough to signal to your interlocutor that they are not important enough to get your undivided attention. This is especially true when you are on a date. If you are interacting with someone whom you are genuinely interested in, it is best to just put the phone away.

One way to get around having a phone on the table is to have it in silent mode. That way you won't be distracted by incoming notifications. However, this is playing with fire as you may still be tempted to check it every once in a while.

As such, you might miss important clues that will lead you to misread the situation, or simply send the wrong message to the object of your interest.

When it comes to advanced body language clues, you really need to pay attention to the subtleties that most folks will let on unconsciously. If you are keen and pay close attention, you can learn a great deal about the people around you. In a way, you can profile your acquaintances by establishing patterns in their behavior. When you get to know someone well enough, it becomes easy to tell when they are lying or hiding something.

Of course, reading a stranger is a bit harder since you have no frame of reference. Nevertheless, the general guidelines which we have discussed up to now ought to provide you with enough fodder to equip you with tools you can use to make sense of the people you encounter on a daily basis.

At the end of the day, the most important thing to keep in mind is that picking up on subtle clues and hints is all a question of practice and experience. Experience is, by far, the most important factor which can enable you to improve your people reading skills.

Furthermore, it is a great idea to keep a journal, even just a simple one, of the behaviors, mannerisms and gestures you find in people. These notes will help you keep specific details in mind especially when you are interested in really getting a good read on someone. Perhaps you are interested in getting a very detailed read on your boss. That way, you can learn to navigate their moods, feelings and even anticipate their reactions.

So, do take the time to make notes on your observations. Your notes will become an invaluable reference down the road especially if you need to influence people around you. Also, notes can help you stay on your toes especially if you are dealing with colorful characters.

Ultimately, your ability to keep your ideas fresh will help you get into a state of readiness in which people's reactions will not catch you off guard. As such, reading people's reactions will become second nature for you. But that all begins with your ability to keep tabs on what others around you are doing. Taking the time to be careful with your notes and observations will pay off in the long run.

# Chapter 7 Mind Control Techniques

**Mind Control in Marketing**

There are many other books concerning mind control, one above all is Dr. Robert Cialdini's *Influence: The Psychology of Persuasion*, that shows clearly the scientific proof of mind control. In the next pages, I focus especially on one important topic: marketing. The most important thing in marketing can be summed up with just one word: YES. If you ask a commercial partner to promote your product, and he or she says "Yes"; if you ask your customers to buy your new product, and they say "Yes"; if you ask a blogger for a link, and he says "Yes," well, then your blog, activity, business is working in the right way and you can really succeed.

And the most important thing here is that you can learn how to do that. Here is a concise guide to mind control. Read it and then use these tips carefully for your advertising and non-business efforts alike.

**Don't let them think for themselves.**

Instead, take charge and do the work yourself. The fact is that people already have too much to think about: job, family, hobbies, friends, children, dogs, and everything else that completely fill people's minds. If you give them something else to think about, they can easily break down or step away from the offer you present altogether. So, it could be a mistake to ask them to think your offer over, even if it's new.

Keep in mind, people usually adjust their focus away from what isn't really important to them, or they just don't think about it very hard. It's not laziness or dumbness, but because they are already too busy and overwhelmed, which makes you as a seller or blogger a pretty low priority.

The first part of this strategy is to not ask them to think, and instead do it for them. Here are some guidelines:

Explain in a clear way how your offer will help, boost, or sustain your audience, show examples of similar situations where your product or service worked well.

Have an idea for an event or learning opportunity? Rather than seeking prep work from your customers, do it for them; plan the event, complementary web pages, and email campaigns needed. Then, provide them with those complete products, with everything already working, and ask for their assistance in finalizing the event.

Online reviews can make or break a product or service. Rather than waiting for customers to write the reviews you need, provide a handful of clear, customizable examples and a strategic list of where they could be posted.

Be specific and clear. Explain yourself and show proof. Tell them exactly what to do step by step and why; and they will be more than happy to tell you "Yes" for everything you are going to ask them.

**Start from a little snowball.**

A successful marketing campaign always starts from something little, to then grow bigger and bigger as things go on. To achieve your ideal "Yes," the hard part is to obtain the first one. But if you get it from the right person, then getting all the other "Yeses" will be very easy. It's like an avalanche, you get a little snowball going down from the top of the mountain and then it becomes a huge and powerful wall of snow. Here are some guidelines:

Try to get someone popular, e.g. a blogger or an influencer, to share your post; however, this is not an easy trip. You may need to practice some reciprocity first, but if they do it just one time, then many other people may retweet, like, or share your post with their followers. And the more time passes, the more it increases.

If you can convince an expert in your field of interest to promote your product or service, then the people who also follow that expert will want to know more about it and be likely to share it, as well.

Again, if you can persuade (maybe with some mind control techniques ?? ) a public figure, or a celebrity, to create a testimonial for your product or service, which is very hard work, then you will see your sales increase so fast you can't even imagine and you will find many other testimonials with little effort.

So, don't be frightened about the hard work you'll have to do at the beginning to get people to help you, because after that, you will see that the road is all downhill and you will begin to see concrete results earlier than you might have imagined.

### Ask for a little thing, take a big one.

Have you ever heard the expression "give them an inch, and they will take a mile"? While it's usually given as advice, a warning against others' greed, it can be great marketing.

If you want to obtain something, don't jump for the whole thing right away. Remember the snowball from point #2 and getting that first "Yes." It's the easiest way to get started, and reduces the risk of wasted time or effort. Then, you can start asking for more (and more, and more) when the results of your effort reveal themselves.

And it's not really unethical, or even manipulation, if you think about it. Why wouldn't you push for more if things are going well? It's not psychological trickery or anything like that; it's just smart business. No one likes to risk everything immediately (maybe just some crazy poker players), and so offering progressive levels of commitment will really increase your chances of making them say "Yes" without any regret.

**Establish a real deadline.**

As you know, deadlines are important because they create a sense of urgency. But always remember: the important thing is that the deadline you set should be *real*.

How many times has a salesman told you to come back as soon as possible when he or she sees that you're not very convinced, maybe telling you that there are other people coming later and you could lose your opportunity by not acting now. This happens so many times in our life. People lie to you or simply pitch you with artificial deadlines, thinking that this will really motivate you to act. Everyone uses this technique: teachers, bosses, wives and husbands. It's very likely you've used this technique, too. The takeaway here? Don't take this ineffective route.

You should, instead, concentrate on generating real urgency. It's not hard, and can be built up with your current marketing plan. For example:

-      If you create content, don't leave free data on your page or blog for an indeterminate time. Consider employing scarcity here, and say that it will be available for a limited time, after which, you will start charging a cost for it. The specific deadline will boost the number of downloads you receive, and fellow bloggers can boost promotion efforts while your report is still free.

-      Rather than waiting for customer testimonials, like we touched on in point #1, let them know there is a precise timeline to respect, especially, that they have to come in by a specific date. Don't think of it as something like a dictatorship, but as helping them be more serious and respectful of the work you are doing for them and for yourself.

**Be generous—give more than you take.**

This concept takes us right back to reciprocity, but the takeaway here is how much you should do. It goes beyond a one-for-one ratio; think ten-to-one. For example, if you're going to ask for a link, you should have already given ten links. If you're going to ask for a promotion, you should have already given ten promotions.

Simply, smart marketers don't resort to a 1:1 ratio; instead, they give ten and take just one. And that goes beyond action; think about value.

If you're going to ask for 100 visitors, you should have already sent 1,000 visitors. If you're going to ask for $1,000 in products or services sales, you should have already sold $10k of their products and services. This is about generosity, and it's a nice way to be sure they always lean closer to "Yes."

And I know it's a lot of work to do, but, trust me, it works and it's worth it. This is the price of influence, and you will see real results and income.

### Support a cause beyond your interests.

Standing for something greater than yourself makes people care. And it can be applied to nearly everything. Rather than write another how-to post, stop and consider writing about an important issue, something you are really passionate about and with a strong logic structure. Thinking of starting another consulting business? You could do something bigger, something that can really change your customers' lives, and lead a movement. From there, you could inspire your customers, take time and write a more important book, about your philosophy maybe. Include many concrete and big examples, maybe about your own life, instead of writing another step-by-step manual.

Those are the kind of things that people want to talk, read, or know about. They will be grateful to you just because you've given them the possibility to help you make the world a better place.

### Make no room for shame.

A great marketer is the one who takes shamelessness as one of the most important principles of gaining influence. And I'm not talking about lacking conscience, or being an extroverted person, or any other stereotype usually connected to how a marketer works. Simply, several of them are just false.

By shamelessness, I mean the resolute belief that what you are doing will benefit the world and the determination to do anything to make it real. When you believe in your products or services, you don't need to lie about them to sell them. Because you really know your products or services can help your customers, and so it becomes a personal duty to share the word, get them to buy, no matter how.

When you believe in your message, you don't just publish and then immediately forget about what you wrote. Instead, you promote your books, your posts, whatever your content, daily, weekly, or even hourly. You will work without stopping to share your content to everyone you think needs it to succeed, and you will refuse to rest until you reach your goal.

It should not be about money, or glory, or legacy. It's about really believing in what you do and say. It's about being charmed, about being so in love with what you do and what it can provide. It's about bringing to life this beautiful vision you have. It's about fighting for what you believe in with every resource you have.

If you really feel this way—well, listen to me—you can achieve nearly anything.

# Chapter 8 Persuasion Techniques to Change the Mind

**Door footstep**:

The door footstep indicates that you should negotiate for a tiny one before applying for a huge one. When you first ask for something small, you are committed to helping the individual, and the greater proposal acts as a reversal of something already agreed on technically.

**Real-life Implementation**: Tourist requests guidance. We suggest that they may get lost and need you to walk there. You agree with that more than if you ask the other question straight away. You lost a class and requested notes from your classmate. You then admit that this semester was very irresponsible and request notes for the whole semester. When you first apply for the tiny favor, the chance of getting the big one improves, a free ride on the notes of your classmate. The professor has not offered a refreshment, and you decide to ask for your feedback and why you have not accompanied by request for a redo. You have only failed. In such a scenario, rather than requesting a recovery, you're more likely to be successful.

**Case study:** In 1966, Jonathan Freedman and Scott Fraser, two researchers at Stánford, decided on a persuasion test to test FITD's effectiveness. One hundred fifty-six women in four groups were divided. The first three groups were called and asked a few basic questions regarding their household kitchen products. We called for their own kitchen cabinet to go and list their items three days later. Only with the second offer was the other group approached. There was an approval rate of 52.8% for the first three teams, while the last class had only 22.2%.

**Door in the face:**

Hey, you'd like to race the roads naked and scream how amazing this chapter is? No? Okay, at least do you post it on Facebook with your buddies? The door to face is the reverse of the above-mentioned method of convincing. First, you ask for anything huge, with which you will not agree, and then ask for something that is, in contrast, easier.

**Real-life implementation**: You are asking a teacher in Advanced Statistics for your next mid-term. Oh, and until now at all, you haven't studied. The student apologizes and says they just have no time. Moreover, never before have they ever seen you. However, your follow-up application for your notes is allowed. You're telling your mate to lend $100 to you. You ask after the No, "can I have a minimum of $20?" A supermarket has a strategy of requiring a charity donation, before requesting the payment from the customer. Although most of our customers would not give money, the number of donations increases exponentially if the Store manager asks them to donate 100 dollars and ask, "How only about 5 dollars."

**Case study:** A study of the DITF technique to support retail sales. Case study: In the Austrian Alps, a saleswoman sold cheese to people passing by a hut. The walkers were decided to offer a pound of cheese for 4 euros in the first scenario.

The saleswomen first provided 2 pounds of cheese for 8 Euros in the second scenario, but after rejection, requested a pound for 4. Compliance rates vary dramatically: 9% for the first application, 24% for the second.

## Anchoring

In most decision-making processes, anchoring is cognitive bias. For instance, how do you understand what "good" product is? You equate it with a similar item, and from there you determine. This technology has many various uses, among which pricing is most commonly used. If properly used, anchoring may be a strong technique of persuasion.

**Real-Life Implementation:** You want to buy a new car and consider an okay price for $10,000. You negotiate with the seller, and you can reduce the cost to $7,000. You go home with satisfaction and disdain, thinking about how much a deal it was. However, the actual value was less than $7,000 for the car. You will receive nothing lower than the initial $10,000 deal as an anchor, so you've only got a new job offer and an initial $2,000 monthly offer. It's about $2,200, which you settle. Once, you could become low-balled, as with the earlier example. Although an increase of 10% over the previous offer might seem attractive, it may still be less than your actual value.

**Case study**: Three separate payment plans were used by the Economist. A) 59 $online printing B) 125 $printing and 125 $printing and web printing. In a 100 MIT study, sixteen chose option A, and 84 chose option C. The experimenter then eliminated Option B and offered the same exam to 100 other participants. Enhance 8 Persuasion tactics to alter everyone's mind 68 selected option A and 32 selected option C in this case.

The takeoff is that people use option B as their anchor. Nobody really would choose it; it was only used to add option C value.

**Commitment & Coherence**

**Principle:** People are more prone to behave and believe regularly. You can use the initial promise to persuade an individual to do more for you if you contribute something little.

**Real-life implementation**: You purchase the same products time and again most of the time. How did you last try a new beverage or snack? "Will you answer me?" You remember." "Can you get me a drink out of the shop? You probably have heard that goal establishing will improve performance. "In comparison," Yeah, you could do, etc. The concept is seldom left out of a book of self-help. It is because of continuity that this is effective: you know more than once you write down this, it's what you want and therefore should strive for. Let's presume you're operating with an NGO, and for some reason, you collect money. You should ask the person to support the cause before asking for money. They would certainly respond favorably if the explanation is right. You are much more likely to receive contributions when posing such a request first.

**Case study**: A lot of websites now use the principle of consistency to make you register for their email lists. They usually read anything in their pop-ups: "Yes, subscribe to me. Free money, I love it!" And" No, I would like not to win. While it might look a little common, it helps to boost conversion rates.

**Social evidence**

**Principle:** This must be real; everybody knows.' Public confirmation is the most compelling tool for argument. It needs little to remember that there is a high degree of group thinking in most social groups. Somebody suggests a concept, and everybody goes with it—even if everyone opposes it. People just look at what their colleagues do and act in the same way before deciding.

**Real-life implementation**: You can consider filling the pot before beginning the change if you have a bare tip jar at work. Customers are much more likely to give feedback if they see an empty tip jar than a full tip jar, so I should actually be doing the same thing. There is a major chance that you could want a Facebook message if it has lots of likes, rather than a post that has none. Social data is the reason why most people consume cigarettes. Everybody cigarettes, and you ought to drink, even though it's safe and with an awful taste.

**Case study**: Many participants were put in a dark room 15 inches from a spot of light in 1935 in an observation made by Muzafer Sherif. The issues were then required to determine how much the object was going. There were different numbers both participants sent. On the next day, the same question was asked and put together. This time, the negotiations began, far from the previous estimates, on a completely different level.

**Authority**

**Principle:** People look to authority in any area or subject, so it can take you a long way to make yourself a link of authority.

**Real-Life application**: If they have been mentioned on major media blogs, many businesses or smaller companies place their "as seen on" icon on their landing pages. When, for instance, one business was on TechCrunch, that implies it's a big deal, since TechCrunch doesn't protect just anybody. 9/10 dentists believe the best one is a certain toothpaste product. It also supplies third world countries with clean drinking water. And heal cancer. In their landing page, organizations tend to discuss their predecessors. It refers in addition to large corporations.

**Case Study**: Where Stanley Milgram, a psychiatrist at Yale University, carried out several psychological studies that were later called Milgram Experiments. The research was conducted in three roles: experimenter, instructor, and subject. The instructor will ask the pupil, the hiring person, questions, who will be the volunteer.

The instructor would deliver an electric shock if the student reacted correctly. Even after the learner "screamed pain," the experimenter continued pushing the teacher to use the electrical shock. In most cases, the teacher only followed the instructions of the experiment, despite being aware that he had caused extreme pain to another man. Even after their students stopped hearing any reaction and assumed that it was over, 8 out of 10 educators proceeded to deliver the shocks. The theft is that most people want to take control over someone, even to do something obviously wrong.

### Scarcity

**Principle:** Scarcity is among the most widely employed salesmen and advertisers' persuasive tactics. People are more likely to want more of the low supply stuff. When you tell others that something is free only for a limited period or that something is in a limited amount, you would rather.

**Real-life implementation**: Booking.com rarely fails to show how only 2-3 spaces were left in the hotel or how 20 people look at the same hotel. Digital marketing companies use scarcity by providing their goods once a year for a certain period while emphasizing the limited time that the product offers. Similarly, offer a discount, but connect a timer or date of validity. The greater the conversion rate, the more you emphasize how restricted the product is. Let's say that you are the salesman at the door. With this tactic of convincing, you can go pretty wild. You might claim, for instance, that you're just in the region that day or that you do a special promotion that is never to be seen. In other terms, at no other point will the consumer be allowed to purchase the item.

**Case study:** 180 participants were split into two classes in an experiment carried out by Luigi Mitton and Lucia Savadori. Next, an item was described that was meant to be rare, and the other was an ample commodity. The experiment reached the conclusion that it was less likely for students to select the good that they were told.

**Reciprocity**

**Principle:** People are often compelled to give back favors. No matter if the person loves the gift, they are inclined to give something back. It is always helpful to feel indebted to you, raising your chances of getting something you really want exponentially.

**Real-Life implementation**: suggest you collect money to help kids find a new home. You might plan a small event until you look for potential sponsors, where children make bracelets from different materials (funny, not the kind of child labor). You can give away the bracelet before requesting a donation so that the possible future donor feels obliged. You probably wouldn't do it if I had questioned you to share this information in the introduction. You are more likely to do so now that you have learned all kinds of useful methods of persuasion, as well as various case studies. Okay?

**Case study**: The more accommodating the waiter appeared, the more the client will pay the experiment carried out in a splendid New York restaurant. The waiter would provide each client with a piece of chocolate in the first case, resulted in an 18% higher tip. In the second, the water will start to walk, turn round, and give the consumer an alternate piece of candy after offering a piece of candy. The result was an increase in the tip to 21%.

# Chapter 9 Influencing People

## Specific Strategies and Tactics

There are tactics that can be utilized so as to make persuasion more successful. All victims are usually presented with different forms of persuasion on a daily basis. A food manufacturing plant will work on getting their victims to purchase a new product, while a movie company will focus on persuading their victims to watch their latest movie projects. These techniques of persuasion will be discussed below:

### Create a need

This is one of the techniques that are often deployed by the persuader so as to be able to get the victim to change their way of thinking. This creates a need or rather appeals to a need that is already pre-existing within the victim. If it is executed in a skilled way, the victim will be eating out of the persuader's palm in no time. What this means is that the persuader will need to tap into the fundamental needs of their victim like for example their need for self-actualization. This technique will in most casework so well for the persuader because the victim is actually going to need these things. Food for example is usually something that we as humans need in order to survive and prolonged lack will pause as a big problem. If the agent can convince the subject that their store is the best, or if they can get more food or shelter by switching their beliefs, there is a higher chance of success.

## Utilizing illustrative and words

The choice of words one chooses to use comes a long way in the success of using persuasion. There are many ways in which you can phrase sentences when actually talking about one thing. Saying the right words in the right way is what will make all the difference when attempting to use persuasion.

## Tricks used by mass media and advertising

The media use two main methods which they use to persuade the masses. First is through the use of images, as well as the use of sounds.

## Media persuasion by use of images

Our sighs and visual processing areas of the brain are very powerful. Just think about it for a minute, have you ever thought of a person without ending up picturing how they look? It is because of this that makes imagery and visual manipulation a preferred method by the media. Companies will often include split-second images of their product or individual inserted into an advertisement that seems quite innocent on the face value. This usually a form of subliminal persuasion. These split-second images that are usually assumed for the most part usually end up taking some form of control of the victim, which persuades them to purchase that particular service.

## Media persuasion by the use of sound

Sound is yet another trick that is used by media in the persuasion of unsuspecting victims. Some people usually underestimate the powers that exist within the sound. But answer me this, how many times have you heard a song somewhere only to have it loops through your mind continuously? Songs usually have an influence on us even though we are not aware of it despite knowing you are listening to it. This is what the media tend to exploit in their quest for persuasion of the masses.

## Persuade Only Those Who Can Be Persuaded

We can all be influenced at one time or another, provided the timing and the context is right. However, for some people, it can take a lot of persuading. Take a look at the politicians and their campaigns - they focus their money and their time almost exclusively on the small percentage of voters who are responsible for determining the outcome of an election. The very first step to successful persuasion is to identify and focus on the people who can, at that moment in time, be persuaded to follow you and your point of view. By doing this, a certain percentage of others - those who can't be persuaded at that moment in time - will be influenced later on to change their course.

## Get Your Timing and Content Right

The timing is what dictates what we are looking for from other people and from life. Often, when we marry, it is to someone very different to whom we may have been dating in our younger years, simply because what we want at any given time is subject to change.

## Uninterested People Cannot Be Persuaded

You simply can't convince people to do something if they genuinely are not interested in what you have to say. In general, the human race is concerned primarily with their own individual selves and most of their time is spent thinking about three things – health, love, and money. The very first step to persuading someone is to learn to talk to that person about themselves. Appeal to their self-interest and you have their attention. Continue to do it, and you will hold their attention for long enough to persuade them.

## Be Persistent but not Overbearing

Take a wander back through history and look at the vast numbers of figures who have persuaded people through persistence, in both message and endeavor.

## Be Sincere in Your Compliments

Whether we admit it or not, compliments do have a positive effect on us, and we are much more likely to place our trust in a person who is sincere and who makes us feel good. Try it – be sincere when you compliment a person, pay them compliments for something that they honestly wouldn't expect it to. Compliment them on something they had to work for: it can be something as simple as their clothing choice. Don't compliment them on their beauty or on other things they were born with. It's quite easy once you learn how to do it, and it costs nothing. The rewards will speak for themselves.

### Set Your Expectations

One of the biggest parts to persuasion is learning to manage the expectations of others when it comes to placing trust in you and your judgment.

### Never Assume

This is a bad mistake to make: to assume what people are looking for. Instead, offer them your value. Take the sales world; often products and services are held back because it is assumed that people simply don't have the money to purchase them, or they have no interest in them. Be bold, get out there and say what you have to offer, say what you can do for them and leave the choice to them. Be persistent, and it will pay off.

### Make Things Scarce

Virtually everything has a value these days, on a relative scale. We need the bare necessities to survive, so they have a far higher value than something we don't need. Often we want something because someone else has it. If you want to persuade people to want what you are offering, it may not be enough to point out the benefits of things or services we are offering. It could be much more effective if we would tell people about its uniqueness and what they could lose. That would create a scarcity feeling, and the less there is, the more people want it. The logic of scarcity is very simple: when something becomes scarce, people want it more.

### Create a Sense of Urgency

If a person doesn't have any real motivation to want something now, they aren't likely to want it later on down the line either. It's down to you to persuade them that time is running out; persuade them now or lose them forever.

### Images are Important

Most people respond better to something they can see. Quite simply if they can see it, then it's real; if you just talk about it, then it might not even exist. Images are potent, and pictures really do speak a thousand words. You don't actually have to use images, just learn how to paint that image in a person's mind.

### Build Up a Rapport

The human race is a funny thing. We tend to like those who are more like us, and this often goes way beyond the conscious into the unconscious. By "copying" or matching your behaviors, regarding cadence, body language, patterns of language, *etc.* you will find that it is easier to build up a rapport with them and easier to persuade them to your way of thinking.

## Real-Life Examples of Influence

### Persuasion in Sales

Persuasion in sales has been going on for as long as people have been selling things. There are so many tactics and systems and efforts geared toward making the sale that it may be one of the most intensely studied one-on-one interactions ever studied. In this section, we'll talk about a few of the Principles of Persuasion can be effectively used to make sales and increase business.

Originally, merchants would give people a free sample of a product, hoping that they would like it enough to want more. Getting people to purchase your product to complete their 'inner story' is as simple as getting them to associate ownership of your product with being the type of person they want to be.

### Persuasion in Marketing

Marketing has now become a sophisticated endeavor that encompasses strategy and behavior studies at many top universities and management consultancies. For our purposes, we'll be including advertising in our marketing mix as well, as they are often close cousins when it comes to persuasion.

### Persuasion in Customer Service

Many business owners think of customer service as a necessary evil, a headache, a pain point. But customer service can be an asset, a chance to lock in future business, and an opportunity to earn positive word of mouth. One way to make sure that customer service interactions go in a positive direction is through using some of the principles and tools of persuasion in all of your dealings with customers, not just when you are trying to get them to buy.

Many times, we need the customer to participate in a solution to a customer service problem. We might need them to send back an item for exchange, or send a picture of a broken part or damaged box.

One idea is to make the process as customer-centered as possible. If your customers feel that you are doing everything you can for them, they are more likely to return the good feeling in cooperation or recommendations to others. Offer a call-back option instead of making people wait on hold, email shipping documents and labels for returns, or give your customers no-wait appointments for help at your location. Showing that you take their time seriously will help you earn their help in return.

### Persuasion in Negotiation

Both negotiation and persuasion share some similarities. In both, you as the persuader or negotiator have a goal to bring someone around to your way of thinking. Where the similarities end may be more in the communication mode used with each. With persuasion, the communication direction is mostly one-way. You come up with your best argument for your position, and you present it in the most effective way possible. You don't get a status report until you reach the end.

With negotiation, on the other hand, both sides are trying to persuade the other, so the communication mode is more two-way. Each party may present part of an argument, only to have part of the other side's argument then presented. Because of this, negotiation tends to be more reactionary out of necessity. It requires the ability to change directions, and adapt our presentation to address the input from the other side.

## Persuasion in Relationships and Sex

Persuasion in close personal relationships can be a tricky business. Nobody likes to be manipulated or be in a relationship where they are not treated as an equal. It's important to focus on respect for the other person you are trying to persuade if you want them to stay in your life. Using persuasion in these areas require that you focus on benefiting the other person while still getting what you want.

We're not suggesting some magical spell that you'll be able to cast over the focus of your attraction that will make them override their own feelings. And we're not talking about mental reprogramming by force. But it never hurts to throw the odds in your favor when it comes to asking for that first coffee. Trying to make sure you do what you can during that first meeting so that he or she is more likely to see you again is not a bad thing. Don't use persuasion to hide your 'true self' from the other person either, because that will show through eventually, and you might both end up miserable. Call these tips a way to put yourself in the best light.

Once you do get a date with that special someone, the same types of subtle mimicry we talked about before can work to your advantage here, too. Adopting a similar sitting posture, for instance, or even some of the same language cues can make you seem more likable. Once people are together for a long time, they start to have these patterns without even thinking about it. You may find you pick up these traits naturally by carefully listening and watching the person you're with.

## Psychological Tactics to Influence People to Do as You Wish

You do not have to be the CEO to motivate individuals to hear you out. The mental research proposes there are a lot of approaches to inspire individuals to do what you need—without them acknowledging you've influenced them. I've gathered together 11 science-supported systems for inspiring individuals to like you, to purchase stuff, and to give you what you're after.

*1. Utilize a "distraction" alternative to inspire individuals to purchase your item.*

In his 2008 TED Talk, behavioral financial specialist Dan Ariely clarifies the "bait impact," providing an old Economist advertisement for an example. The advertisement included three membership levels: $59 for online, $125 for print only, and $125 for on the web and print. Ariely made sense of that, noting the choice to pay $125 for print only exists so it makes the choice to pay $125 for on the web and print look more alluring than it would on the off chance that it was so closely matched with the $59 choice.

As a final decision in the end, in case you're experiencing difficulty offering the more costly of two items, consider including a third alternative whose lone capacity is to make the "costly" item look all the more tempting.

*2. Change the environment to inspire individuals to act.*

"Priming" is an effective mental marvel in which one stimulus delivers an associated reaction to another stimulus, frequently unwittingly.

One example, referred to in the book *You Are Not So Smart*, found that members playing an ultimatum game selected to keep more than half of a cash prize for themselves when they were situated in a room with business-related items like a satchel, a calfskin portfolio, and a fountain pen versus when people were asked to connect items with unbiased associations, like a backpack, a pencil, and cardboard box. Despite the fact that none of the members knew about what had happened, the business-related articles may have primed those subjects of the game to be more selfish.

This strategy could possibly work when you're dealing with somebody one on one, as opposed to meeting in a gathering room, consider assembling in a coffeehouse, so your audience is less disposed toward animosity.

*3. Help propel somebody's objectives to motivate them to help you.*

Analyst Robert Cialdini says one approach to impact individuals is to conjure the correspondence standard, invoking the concept of reciprocity. Essentially, you help somebody with something they require, so they feel obliged to furnish a proportional payback.

What's more, when gratitude has been expressed for your assisting, Cialdini exhorts saying something like, "Obviously, it's what accomplices accomplish for each other," rather than "It's no issue," so they have a feeling that they're relied upon to do likewise for you.

*4. Copy individuals' non-verbal communication to inspire them to like you.*

Whenever you're attempting to awe an enlisting administrator or to offer a protestation of your love, attempt unobtrusively mirroring the way they're sitting and talking—they'll presumably like you more. Researchers call it the "chameleon effect": we tend to like discussion partners that copy our stances, idiosyncrasies, and outward appearances.

The weirdest part of this phenomenon is that it generally happens unknowingly—most members in the "chameleon effect" study weren't even mindful that they were being duplicated.

*5. Talk rapidly to get a contentious rival to concur with you.*

How you impart your thoughts can be as vital as the substance of your contention. There are recommendations that when somebody can't help contradicting you, you ought to talk quicker, so they have less time to process what you're stating enough to respond.

Expectedly, when you're conveying a contention that your audience concurs with, talk more gradually, so they have an opportunity to assess the message.

*6. Confound individuals to inspire them to agree to your demand.*

The "disrupt-then-reframe" (DTR) procedure is a subtle approach to inspire individuals to participate. One review found that when experimenters visited individuals' homes offering note cards for philanthropy, DTR helped them profit when they were offering eight cards for $3; as in the DTR fashion, they told individuals it was 300 pennies for eight cards, "which is a deal."

Analysts say that DTR works because it upsets routine manners of thinking. While attempting to make sense of what number of dollars 300 pennies turns out to, individuals are occupied. Thus, they simply acknowledge the possibility that the cost is actually "a deal."

*7. Approach individuals for favors when they're drained to inspire them to participate.*

A ready personality may express some uncertainty when tasked with a demand. However, somebody who's drained or occupied will probably be less unsure, and will basically acknowledge what you say as genuine.

So, if you want to request that a colleague assists with a venture that will, as far as anyone knows, just take 60 minutes, it's best to solicit toward the end of the workday. That way, they'll be depleted from the day's assignments and won't have the mental vitality to understand that the venture will likely take up a greater amount of their time.

*8. Show a picture of eyes to inspire individuals to carry on morally.*

In one review, individuals were more compelled to tidy up after themselves in a cafeteria where they saw a picture of eyes than when they saw a picture of blossoms. The review creators say that eyes normally invoke the idea of social investigation.

Regardless of whether you're attempting to avoid littering or urge individuals to give back the books they obtain from the workplace library, it gives individuals the feeling that they're being viewed.

*9. Utilize nouns rather than verbs to inspire individuals to change their conduct.*

In one review, individuals were solicited for responses to two adaptations of a similar question: "How imperative is it for you to vote in tomorrow's decision?" and "How critical is it to you to be a voter in tomorrow's race?" Results demonstrated that members in the "voter" condition will probably cast their ballot at the polls the following day.

This is likely on the grounds that individuals are driven by the need to have a place, and utilizing a noun fortifies their way of life as an individual from a group.

*10. Panic individuals to motivate them to give you what you require.*

Collected research proposes that individuals who encounter uneasiness followed by a liberating sensation, as a rule, react emphatically to subsequent demands. For instance, individuals who heard an undetectable policeman's shriek while crossing the road were more likely to consent to take a survey than individuals who didn't hear anything.

This phenomenon is justifiable and understood in light of the fact that their subjective processing assets were preoccupied pondering the potential threat they experienced, so they had fewer assets left to consider the light demand (i.e., the survey) that was recently postured.

*11. Focus on what your bartering associate is gaining to motivate them to take your offer.*

While bartering, accentuate for your associate what they're going to gain instead of what they're losing by taking your offer. For instance, if you're attempting to sell a used automobile, you ought to state, "I'll give you my car for $1,000," rather than, "I need $1,000 for the car."

That way, your associate could understand the offer as being made from an "I'm about to cut you a deal" point of view, and they'll presumably use that gain to justify the purchase.

# Chapter 10 Advanced Sales Triggers and Psychological Tricks

### How To Sell Without Losing Your Soul

Being a salesperson isn't easy. Even more difficult is to be an ethical salesperson who would sell without losing his or her soul. No one would believe a fake salesperson that puts on the charade of knowing you the moment they meet you. You would be shocked to know how the modern buyer is smart and knowledgeable.

So, instead of using your fake demeanor to sell, resort to some genuine counseling of your customer's need and sell the product out of his willingness. Believe in establishing a mutual and cordial relationship with your buyer without imposing yourself.

Here are some ways to be a likeable salesperson who believes in sane and rationale selling unlike those pushy ones who have gone redundant:

### #1 Let Selling be not just Selling; solve a problem

The buyers are smart enough to gauge your mindset. They can sense if it is tilted towards hardcore selling or genuine for earning their loyalties. You don't have to focus on the word selling. Rather, take yourself as a guide who is going to help people in finding what they precisely need. This way, you would be able to understand the needs of your customers and appeal to their preferences.

### #2 Do not be hell bent on selling

The harder you are trying to sell, the farther will your buyers be, out of distrust and doubt. Let the whole process of selling and buying be forgotten and lay stress on how you can help the customers. Trust me, it is going to show in your body language and you would end up being in the trusted books of your buyers. This would consequently help you in recommending your own product or service and customers will believe you easily.

If you want to be a successful sales person, you need to be honest and as natural as possible when trying to make a sale.

### #3 Start slow and steady

As a salesperson, you may be a smooth talker. Talks and reasons may come to you effortlessly and you enjoy narrating them. However, selling is not all about ranting about what we know.

On meeting a prospective buyer, DO NOT even mention what you are selling during the first ten minutes. If you want to start talking about your product, prospective buyers will simply shut you out and no matter what you say, they are not going to buy anything.

Ideally, let your customers speak and listen carefully to know what they want. Your initial silence will go a long way in making the customer feel that you are really interested in helping them out if you can hear them out.

## #4 Express instead of impress

Instead of impressing your customers be expressive and derive the same out of them. Do not use too much sales jargon such that they have to interpret your sales data. Rather, keep your selling approach simple and effortless. Shun the belief that buyers make their mind after watching glossy or flashy presentation. Rather, it makes them distracted from the real profile of the product.

## #5 Create an irresistible offer

There are plenty of products or services out for sale on various platforms. To make your product outstanding, you have to offer what others haven't or cannot. If a product is sold for $200 and you are selling it for $200 only, no rampage would take place. Try selling the same product for just $199 and you will be amazed at how people can do everything to save even that $1.

## #6 Take after-sale responsibility

Most of salespersons are usually just quick to sell you a product without even taking after-sales responsibility. This is a clear demarcation between a good and a bad salesperson. In order to carry on ethical selling, one simply cannot remain alienated from what happens to the product or service after the selling point.

Selling should include a satisfying experience that would come if the seller guides the buyers over after-sale problems. There needs to be effective interaction via feedback forms so that customers can give their feedback or ask for after-sales service.

## #7 Guarantee quality or money back

One simple way to sell without losing your soul is to either deliver quality or return a customer's hard earned money. The money-back policy works like a charm, as the customer decides to try without any pitfalls for him. A smart seller would not just sell a product but also rather sell the end result that would endorse their product even further. Buyers will then get comfortable and fearless in buying.

## #8 Sell without being devious

Selling without any devious methods helps in building long term bonds. Once buyers are convinced about getting quality products or services from you, they will definitely become loyal customers. Don't just concentrate on 'selling'. Make your selling a worthwhile opportunity that will empower the buyer with a quality product.

For example, you have with you a costly silk carpet with intricate embroidery. In a city, it would be priced for more than several thousand dollars. Now you took it to countryside and sold it for $200 worth of terracotta pots. The potter may feel happy to get such an exotic carpet. Actually, this deal is completely absurd and futile, since the carpet has no or little value to the potter and is likely to remain hidden in their storage area. As a salesperson, you do not qualify as making an ethical or sensible deal.

Let us rewind the situation and assume that you gave an automated potter's wheel worth $100 to that potter in exchange of his terracotta pots. Now, this would be a sensible deal for the potter, as that automated wheel will help him in making many more pots in the future. He would be able to obtain a lot more value from the product you sold him for many years to come.

## Consider all possibilities

The very fact that you have a brilliant idea does in no way imply that you are 'sorted' when it comes to being on the path to entrepreneurial success. You have to understand that there will be a lot of hurdles along the way, which could indeed lead to a lot of disappointment should things go askew in the process of setting up that business.

Of course you need to be mentally prepared for the same; the last thing you want is to be discouraged by the potential hurdles that come along your path, to the point where you want to throw it all away.

By being apprised of the hurdles that might come along, you are preparing yourself to be a lot more resilient than you otherwise would have been, thus paving the way for you to face any obstacle that might come your way. In fact, some of the most successful entrepreneurs out there are those that have embraced failure time and again, simply because they believed to the core in the ideas that they felt would change the world.

Of course it is vital that you have a great business idea to begin with. Sometimes you might just get that 'Eureka!' moment when you're sitting in a mall and observing things around you. But in addition to the pointers that we have discussed, one also needs to do a thorough amount of research into the idea that they have stumbled upon, in order to assess its viability in the market out there.

**Loading the Funnel**

**Always Be in Contact**

People have often said that sales are a numbers game. Put enough leads in the pipeline, and eventually, sales will come out of the other end. That's only partially true.

In most cases, sales is a *contact* game; not the kind of contact where you need a helmet (hopefully!), but the kind of contact that keeps you in regular communication with your clients and potential clients. In this chapter, we'll talk about how to keep in contact with your prospects and clients, so that your sales funnel is always full of potential deals just waiting for you to close them.

### *The Most Important Sales Call*

No matter what you're selling, there is no more important contact that you will make with a prospective customer than the *first* contact. Sometimes known as a "cold call," this first contact is the toughest part of the job for most salespeople. Sure, there are several important points in a sales cycle, but where you need to be on your A-game is when you first make contact with a new client.

If you are selling in a system that gives you warm leads to work from, congratulations! Most sales professionals don't have that luxury, especially in highly competitive industries or markets. What your company has given you is a gift, and you should take it and run.

Warm leads are contacts where a customer has requested contact because they are ready to buy. They are just trying to decide where. That is a long way down the funnel, so you have an advantage toward moving into a sale.

But, that doesn't mean that your first contact is any less important. It could be argued that your first customer meeting is even *more* important since much more work has already been done for you. It would be a shame to fumble the client contact when you are already this close to winning.

For those of you who have leads that are simply names on a list, you may have more work to do to convert the sale, but your first call is even more important to your success. Without getting that lead to at least start the journey with you, you are out of luck.

Either way, understanding the principles of persuasion and being able to put them to work for you is vital for any first customer contact. Don't waste your first impression. Use it instead to set up your success.

The easiest first call persuasion tactic is to use Reciprocity. Find something that you can give to the customer in the first few seconds of the call; if you make the whole purpose of that first contact about giving the customer something, even better. Your generosity will set them up to give you something in return later in this call or the next, and the thing you are looking for is an agreement to meet again. That "yes" also begins to lay the groundwork for Consistency, getting the customer to start a history of agreeing with you.

The whole point of this first contact should be to get the customer to like you, and the easiest way to do that on the first contact is not to waste their time. Since the first contacts usually happen on your schedule and not the customer's, you should respect their time.

Even if you are selling something that is fairly low cost, where your first contact might be the opening to a single sales call, you still need to establish Liking right up front. It may be the only way to keep the customer talking to you.

No matter the situation, the last thing you want to do in your opening contact is to try and sell. Instead, use some quick efforts at persuasion to keep the conversation moving to the next step.

### The Importance of Follow-Up

If the first contact is the most important part of the sales cycle, then follow up is the second. Before you leave the first contact stage, your effort should be to do no more than setting up a commitment for the follow-up.

Recapping quickly on what we've done so far setting up your persuasion track, you'll note we've already talked about the principle of Consistency, and how important it is to get the client moving in your direction. Setting up Reciprocity by giving something early also puts you in a good position for success on your next contact as well. Thanks to these early persuasion techniques you've implemented, the follow-up should be an easy next step.

Depending on your product and situation, your follow-up could take several different forms. Next are some ideas on where you could head during the follow-up. Consistency and Reciprocity both suggest that this is a good time to ask for your first "yes." Not a big ask, but something the customer can agree to, followed by permission to schedule an in-depth needs analysis.

### *Position Yourself as an Ongoing Resource*

By positioning yourself as a resource for your customer, you will accomplish two things where persuasion is concerned. First, you can continue the Consistency principle that you've started in your first contact by continuing to provide value for your client. Once they build a habit of depending on you for your expertise, they will start to make you the first call for any questions they have in your industry. This status puts you first in line for the new business going forward. Even if the client calls you for a solution that you don't provide, it's better to get to make that decision. Who doesn't want the "right of first refusal" on new business?

With Consistency established with this customer, when you do have something you can sell them, they will already be primed for the "yes." Here's where the investment in persuasion pays off. Customers who buy before are more likely to continue to buy from you, without reinvesting more time.

Next, you can use the persuasion principle of Authority through your ongoing contact by making *yourself* the authority. Building your profile with your clients by passing on interesting information, new product tips and demos on products you think could help them will make your recommendations be the deciding factor in future buying choices. Even if the information you give doesn't directly have anything to do with the product you sell, making yourself an authority in the space will make sure that you know anytime the customer is ready to make a purchase. That early contact will give you a chance to make alternative or complementary suggestions from your product line.

### Selling is a Continuous Process

Selling is not so much of an individual task as it is a continuous process. While you may be finishing a sale with one client, you may also be making the first contact with some new prospects and checking in with your existing customers. Here are some thoughts on managing the constantly moving sales cycle.

### *Use Your Contact to Uncover Needs*

As sales professionals know, you need to be in contact early and often in your prospect's sales journey. Early contact is important from a persuasion standpoint as well. The best time to use your persuasion techniques is during the initial part of the sales cycle so that you can have things moving your way by the time the customer is ready to write the check.

Keeping in contact at the early part of the sales funnel also allows you to find additional needs that may change the sale in your favor or give you an additional sale with add-ons or upgrades.

Your sales process should include a lot of listening and just enough talking to keep the conversation going. Information is the absolute gold you're looking to uncover if you are going to be able to take maximum advantage of your persuasion opportunities.

The problem is that most people don't naturally give up information or talk at all without prodding. The key to keeping the other side of the conversation going is to talk as little as possible, giving important information and asking open-ended questions.

Many salespeople like to talk and this works against you. Learn to listen and react to what your client is telling you about their needs. No two people buy for the same reasons, and by listening to the needs of each particular customer, you can use the principles of persuasion to your best ability.

## *Address Needs and Position Yourself as the Expert*

Perfecting your abilities as a strong listener allows you to address the needs of your customer head-on, instead of only finding out about a particular question your client may have when you get down to signing the check.

In addition to answering the customer's concern and removing barriers to the sale, you can also use these opportunities to engage persuasion more in your favor. Let's take a look at each of the persuasion principles and see where they can be effectively applied to addressing the needs of your customer and moving them farther down the funnel toward the sale.

### Reciprocity

Remembering that the principle of Reciprocity says that you are more likely to get something back if you first give something of value, taking the time to thoroughly address concerns will earn you a lot of payback later in the sales process. Make sure that you highlight your desire to take care of their questions and not rush them into a decision without all of the facts. This attention to making them feel comfortable will translate into more willingness to move through the final sales process quickly later.

### Scarcity

Many times, you will have the ability to note how a particular feature or benefit of your product is something only your offering provides. Being the only one to offer an answer to a question or need that the customer has can give you a real 'no brainer' status on the list of possible choices.

But how can you use Scarcity if your offering isn't the best at addressing a customer concern? Focus the conversation on the scarcity of a certain price or availability to push past the reluctance to accept your answer. "We offer solid performance on that point, similar to most everybody in the market, but this limited time pricing offer makes us by far the best value if you make your purchase now."

## Authority

When your customer comes up with questions, you should have facts and information from third-party sources whenever possible. Keeping a virtual clipping file that you can email at a moment's notice is great for showing what industry publications and well-known customers have said about your product, especially in situations that directly address the customer's question.

Read trade magazines and set web clipper alerts for various questions that you get asked often and collect authoritative answers that will back you up on key points.

## Consistency

Have some options at the ready to address concerns during the sales cycle. Presenting these options as a question of "which will work better for you" will keep the customer selecting you and your product. There is no wrong answer in this type of scenario since it is merely a choice of *how* they wish to buy, not *if*. "I understand you need for more capacity. We have an option for larger 7-gallon and 12-gallon tanks. Which would work best for you?" Selecting either one is saying "yes" again, which is a pattern you want to reinforce at every step.

## Liking

One of the more obvious points, but treating the client with the kind of respect they appreciate will only make you like them more. A purchase can be a high-stress time for many people, especially when the dollar amount is large. Never lose track of that, and use your answers to questions to make the customer feel that they are being thoughtful in their decision-making, letting them know that you appreciate the time they are putting into making the right decision.

## Consensus

Here it's good to have your clipping file at the ready to show what "most people" do in similar situations. Subconsciously, people want to be part of the crowd. Use opportunities to reinforce that with answers to questions. "Most of my customers go with the three-year service plan to cover that type of use." "The company sells the 72-inch wide version almost three-to-one because a lot of people need that same capacity."

<u>Unity</u>

Make sure that you take time during this part of the process to point out where the customer is thinking like you, highlighting how you are similar to the customer. The principle of Unity says that people tend to buy from people that are "like them," so use questions and concerns to highlight that. "I went with that same model when I bought mine." "I wondered that, too, so I did a little digging in the specs and here's what I found." Always try to point out that you are on their side in this process.

### *Prospect, Sell, Follow Up*

As long as your customer is in the decision-making process, they are in the funnel and still moving toward a potential sale. This thinking is what's behind that well-worn adage of 'prospect, sell, and follow-up.' In the days of limited information, expensive travel and difficult contact, the salesman who won the sale was often the guy or gal who showed up over and over and over again.

Today is a different story. Your customer is inundated with contact from a variety of sources all day, every day. Just making contact isn't enough anymore. Every sales pro, including your competition, can do that easily while making your customer feel like they don't want to think about this decision anymore. But you can't lose contact with the customer and potentially lose the sale to someone else. Follow-up is still highly important to closing the sale. It just needs to be done with persuasion in mind.

Sales guru Jill Konrath agrees with this need to re-think the follow-up system you may be using and work to add value to each contact. Her tips include re-iterating the value your product or service will bring to their situation, sharing thoughts and insights you may have had regarding the customer's situation since your last meeting, and using your repeat contact opportunities to educate your customer further.

I find that education is the one thing that you can always offer your customer that adds value for the customer while giving you further persuasion advantages. Educating the customer further cements your Authority with the customer, gives you a Reciprocity advantage, and builds Liking for you, to name just a few of the persuasive points. So, let's take a moment to focus on how you can make education work for you to close the sale.

### Always Have Something to Give

Because follow-up and continued customer education can add such persuasive punch to your sales process, it's important to be thinking about this before you ever make your first prospecting call. It's vital to have resources that you have planned to use for this purpose, just as it will be important that you continue to build these resources on a regular basis so that you always have something to give.

In the remainder of this chapter, we'll talk about some ideas of what you can develop at little to no cost. No matter what cooperation your company may or may not give you, you can still create value for your customers to keep them moving toward the sale.

## *Organize Events or Meet-ups*

Always have something to invite people to. This one change in sales strategy can double your business inside of a year.

Principles of persuasion tell us that Reciprocity is important to foster in our customers, and giving something helps to get something later in return. This is one of the reasons that having events to invite people to regularly is a low-cost or no-cost way to give your customers something of value that will undoubtedly have a positive impact on your business. Who doesn't like to be invited to something relevant to them or their business?

What kind of event could you create? Imagination is the key. The most obvious is the open house night to allow customers to get hands on your products or get expert advice on how to use them. If you sell forklifts, you could invite clients to come and try out some of the inventory in the warehouse or the parking lot. If you sell gas grills and outdoor cooking equipment, you could invite a local barbecue chef in to give some cooking tips and make some food. (Everybody shows up for free food!)

Meet-ups are free and easy to set up. Come up with a topic related to your business and set a Meet-up date for a local restaurant's banquet room for lunch. Open it up to the public on Meetup.com and promote it to all of your customers. You might end up with new prospective customers you haven't met yet! You might want to pick up the tab for a couple of key customers to come; most will pay their own way for the chance to learn more about the subject you're speaking about.

Meetings don't have to be in person, either. Consider webinars and conference calls or even recorded video presentations that you've held previously. And of these ideas and many others would be an opportunity to keep in contact with a prospective customer without needing to push the sale. All the while, you not only increase Reciprocity in your side of the ledger but you also further your Authority and Liking persuasion as well.

### Develop Resources

Developing your educational resources doesn't need to cost anything more than your time if you can manage the word processing program or presentation software. If you're not a wizard with this type of thing, you can get help relatively inexpensively from online job sites like Fiverr, Upwork and Freelancer. Just put some notes together with what you want and send them off. Once created, you only need to keep these items updated to keep them current and valuable to use time and time again.

What types of things could you produce? Keep notes on questions you hear from customers regularly, and come up with information to answer the questions. Then, find unique ways to put this information into a form that you can easily distribute via email or a download site like Dropbox or Google Drive.

Powerpoint slides can be combined with your voice to create an informative video. Typing up a print report can be formatted into a professional looking PDF white paper or even a short book that will be perfect to pass out to customers.

There are even options for creating micro websites for free, such as Google Sites, allowing you to assemble a website page quickly by dragging and dropping various elements around a page. If you can set up a Powerpoint slide, you've got this. Spreadsheets, charts, artwork, audio; almost anything you can think of can be created and distributed digitally.

You don't even need to go to this much effort for everything. Almost anything can be a valuable resource for a customer if it answers a question. Making a habit of checking the web every day for interesting articles may give you just the opening you need to send an email to a customer that day. "I know you've been trying to decide on which model to go with, and I just saw this article on the 9000 that I thought might give you some more good information."

### *Partner with Other Businesses for Gifts and Perks*

In your contact with customers, you are bound to run into other products and services that they are also buying that complement your product. Keep track of these other companies who don't compete with you, but sell to the same customers. Make contact with these other companies and offer to partner up to help both of you. If they have information or discounts that you can give to your new customers, work with them to pass on these leads to their salespeople. While you're at it, offer some of the giveaway items that you've developed for an opportunity to talk to their customers as well.

Working in partnership with other non-competing businesses can be a win-win for both of you, plus it gets more valuable information to your customers and gives you another reason to make contact during the sales process. From a persuasion standpoint, showing cooperation from other businesses elevates your profile as an expert even more and shows consensus with other members of the industry. Passing on information from another company can provide their indirect approval to show your prospective client that others respect your business as well.

# Chapter 11 Self-Persuasion and How to Exploit it on Others

In this chapter, you will discover detailed persuasion techniques that give you the ability to persuade others to perform some action or believe some idea.

### The Freedom to Say No

If you want somebody to go along with your suggestion, they must first get the impression that they have the freedom to reject it. Request the thing that you want of the other person, and then remind them that they have the freedom to decline. For example, you might say to your acquaintance, "You can totally say no, but can I have one of those beers in your cooler?" Your nonchalant, non-expectant attitude will not only make the other person more likely to comply, it will also make them like you more as you display your ability to get rejected. They are likely to say yes because humans have a desire to please the people (and animals) that they like.

Performing this gambit will give the person on the other end of the conversation the impression that you do not expect anything out of them, and thus will more likely appreciate anything that they do give you. The ways in which you phrase this technique do not matter so much as do its implications. You can use phrases like "But please don't feel obligated" and "Don't feel like you have to." Communication scholars generally agree that only seven percent of communication is verbal, so a genuine tone will help this gambit's effectiveness more than an eloquently strung together combination of words will.

### Reciprocation

If you hold a door open for somebody, they feel obligated to say thank you.

This technique takes advantage of the fact that humans feel obligated to help someone out in the future if they receive a favor or gift from that person. In many cultures, customs dictate that people bring gifts to the host of a gathering in exchange for their hospitality. So, you can make somebody feel indebted to you by doing something nice for them.

For example, charities often give away flowers in the airports where they solicit donations. The thoughtfulness implied in the flower giveaway lends itself to more donating. Amusingly, travelers often throw these flowers away shortly after they receive them. The charity workers then collect the discarded flowers, only to give them away again to the next flock of travelers.

One study conducted in a fancy restaurant in New York found that a server who gave complimentary candy to his diners received significantly higher tips than he did when he neglected to give out candy. His tips increased even more when he then let the diners choose a second piece.

So, if you want to prompt somebody to do something for you, first go out of your way for them. Of course, reciprocation works both ways; if another being makes an effort on your behalf, ask if you can do anything for them. You might just develop a friendly relationship based on reciprocal favors.

**Foot in the Door**

The foot in the door technique gets its name from the idea that you must step your foot inside of a doorway before you can pass your whole body through. Similarly, successfully asking someone to comply with a smaller request first will increase the likelihood that they indulge you with a bigger favor. Think of the small request as your foot, and the weightier favor as the rest of your body.

For example, one study found that a man, one at a time, asked hundreds of women for dates. All of these women were strangers to him. He received five times more yesses when he began his interactions by asking for directions or to borrow a lighter than he did when the date was his first request.

You might utilize this technique by asking a coworker for a stick of gum before you ask them to cover your upcoming shift. You might ask your professor to look over your report's first draft before you ask for a deadline extension.

Video games make use of the psychology behind the foot in the door technique when they "ask" players to complete easy levels before requiring them to complete more difficult stages.

I witnessed a panhandler use this gambit firsthand. As I was pulling out of the parking lot of a strip mall, I noticed an elderly man displaying a hand-written cardboard sign that bore a request for donations. I had a few quarters in my ashtray, so I took sympathy on the guy and reached across my car and outside of my passenger side window to give him two quarters. He thanked me, and then asked for two more! "I just saw you had them sitting there," he went on. It worked, as I sort of obliged and gave him one more before I said goodbye and drove myself home.

This technique will not help persuade anyone to comply with wholly unreasonable requests. For example, asking a stranger to load your bulky furniture into a moving truck before asking them to buy you a car will, most likely, get you nowhere.

For a humorous take on this concept, see Laura Numeroff's illustrated children's publication *If You Give a Pig a Pancake.*

### Mild Confusion + Reframe

Usually, when humans communicate, they carry expectations about the ways in which their conversational partners organize their thoughts into words. This two-step technique involves disrupting one's expectations of language and then reframing their mind in the moment of distraction. It is used to subtly influence another person while their guard is down as they work out the mild confusion.

Start by phrasing the next sentence in your conversation in a slightly odd manner. For example, instead of telling a potential customer that a certain item costs "five dollars," tell them that it will cost them "five hundred pennies." Then, while they try to figure out the more plain language version of what you just said, offer them a good reason for complying with you. For example, in that moment, you might say something like "I'm offering you a bargain." Individuals are more susceptible to persuasion while they are in a state of confusion. Confused individuals have trouble making sense of their immediate situation and are more likely to rely on others to make sense of it for them. By guiding their thoughts along after you mildly confuse them, you stand to persuade them.

Timing is essential for the success of this technique. If you wait too long after your oddly stated phrase induces mild confusion, then your conversational partner will be again fully capable of guiding their own thoughts by the time you get around to the reframing step. Give the reason for complying before they wholly make sense of your strangely said sentence.

## Authority

Those with legitimate authority can persuade others to act, regardless of the suggested action's morality. To use an extreme example, Adolf Hitler persuaded his officers to execute millions of minorities in Europe. More recently, one study found that participants would willingly administer increasingly painful shocks to another subject if the researcher told them to. It did not matter how much the shock receivers screamed; around eighty percent of participants complied with the researcher's orders. Why? Because he was in a position of authority.

Even today, high-ranking military officials persuade their subordinates to kill people from other nations. Authority is an immensely powerful tool of persuasion that can and often does have fatal consequences if the wrong people exercise it.

Do not think of this technique's application as inherently evil. It has application in non-violent contemporary settings as well. Managers and bosses use their authority to persuade employees to perform at a certain level. Security guards use their authority to persuade concert attendees to behave in accordance with the venue's rules. If you want to better persuade others, earn yourself a legitimate position of authority.

## Door in the Face

Not to be confused with the foot in the door technique, this gambit involves asking for a sizable request, and then asking for a much smaller request. One classic example of this technique in action centers on a man in a bar who wants other people to pay for his drink. He makes his way around the inside of the venue, asking every single customer to pay for his cocktail. Naturally, every one of them declines or refuses. When they refuse to pay for the drink in full, however, he presents them with a much more reasonable request: he asks the customer to spare him a few coins. Most customers oblige him, and the man pays his tab in nickels and dimes without ever using any of his own money.

## Legitimizing Miniscule Favors

If you can make people feel like their contributions count, even if those contributions are largely insignificant, then they are more likely to contribute more significantly. After all, if a small favor puts someone in your good graces, what would a large favor do?

Use this technique to get people to do what you want. This technique involves making another person's miniscule contributions to your cause, whatever that may be, come across as meaningful and legitimately helpful. For example, charities often use this technique when soliciting donations from individuals and organizations. Their pitches include phrases like "every penny counts." Furthermore, panhandlers make use of this psychology when they hold up handmade signs that read "anything helps."

So, if you want somebody to perform a small task or favor for you, let them know how much it would mean to you. You might ask for help with your cooking routine by telling your neighbor "Hey, I'm super busy today and <u>it would really mean a lot to me</u> if you could let me bum an egg off you."

You could even further practice your persuading by following up with the "The Freedom to Say No" gambit from earlier in this chapter. For example, after making your request in which you legitimize their egg lending, tell them "But I totally understand if not." Remember that subtlety rules persuasion, however.

## Low-Balling

Low-balling is a persuasion technique in which one makes a request with the intention of adding additional clauses to that request once the request has been agreed to. For example, imagine that a salesperson gets a client to agree to buy a product for $9.00. At this point, the client is sold and committed to making the purchase. Before any money is exchanged, the salesperson informs that client of a $1.00 processing fee, bringing the total up to $10.00. The client would most likely agree to this clause and pay ten dollars. Why? The client has already settled on their decision to buy from the salesperson. Cancelling the sale would create a cognitive dissonance within the client. (A cognitive dissonance describes the uneasy feeling that one gets when their actions do not align with their thoughts and beliefs).

## Anchoring

Anchoring involves comparing one thing to another similar thing. Salespeople will use this technique when they compare their product to similar offerings on the market, and then explain why the product that they sell is so much better. Customers perceive the salesperson's product as superior, and thus think that they must be making a relatively sound investment if they buy the salesperson's product.

Alternatively, salespeople and marketers anchor prices. To illustrate, consider the sticker price of a new car. If a new car has a sticker price of $22,000, it will seem like a good bargain when the salesman offers it to you for $18,000. The car may be worth less than $18,000, but it still seems like a deal because that price is anchored to the much higher sticker price.

How can you use this technique to get something out of another person? Anchor your request to a much larger favor that somebody else did for you. For example, imagine that you want an unfamiliar acquaintance to let you stay a night on their couch in the middle of your long road trip. Before you mention what you want, tell the other person about a recent time when a total stranger let you a place to stay for an entire week when you had nowhere else to go. Then, relative to your weeklong couch surfing endeavor, one night of hospitality will seem like nothing more than a mild inconvenience, if at all a type of burden. Of course, ethics dictate that you avoid making up stories for the purpose of getting what you want, but this is not a book on ethics.

## Social Proof

Social proof refers to the idea that if everyone else likes or does something, then you should like or do it, too. Studies show that a man surrounded by beautiful women is perceived as more attractive than that same man sitting alone is. Most people would rather go along with a group dynamic than go their own route and implicitly disagree the decisions of a social group. You can make use of this principle in everyday life.

For example, if you have a tip jar at your job, consider putting a few bills and coins in it before your shift starts. This will generate more tips than will an empty tip jar. People think that if other customers leave tips, then they probably should as well.

Peer pressure works because of this technique's psychology. Many young people feel obligated to drink or use tobacco because of the number of their peers who engage in the same vices. In many cases, these substances have been socially proven within the social group of teens and young adults who try them for the first time.

### Scarcity

People can be prompted to take action if they believe that their opportunity for doing so will not exist in the near future. By placing limitations on one's opportunity to act, they will feel compelled to seize their chance before it goes away.

Think about the last infomercial you saw. Chances are, it included a line that implies scarcity. Infomercials tend to include phrases like "order in the next fifteen minutes to receive this bonus offer" or "quantities are limited." The truth is, these phrases carry little weight. You will receive the bonus offer no matter when you call, because it is always available. The infomercial's producers throw this clause into their ad and figure that if a customer asks for the bonus, then it was probably within fifteen minutes of the last time the advertisement aired on some station. The producers imply scarcity, compelling potential customers to make the decision to buy at that moment, rather than wait for the right time.

How can you make use of the scarcity technique in your life? Suppose you want to persuade another individual to go out on a date with you tonight. Imply scarcity by telling him or her that this is your last night in town. Or, perhaps you are trying to sell your car. You have the right customer lined up; you just need him to commit to the sale. Imply the scarcity of your offer by telling him that a dozen other people are interested in buying the vehicle. No matter your cause, scarcity acts as a powerful motivator.

# Conclusion

Congratulations, my friend, you've made it to the end. I'm sure that you now have a clear understanding of what influence is. Remember that influencing people isn't necessarily an evil or bad thing. In the end, what you're really doing is persuading them to look at the world from your point of view. There are benefits in this both for them and for you. It's a win-win!

You may need to apply different strategy to different people at different places. At times your strategy of thinking only to close a sale and get the customer agree to buy could work out. But at the same time, it is not good to force the customer to buy something just for the heck of it. While your intention is to make the customer buy what you sell, it should be in a way they are comfortable with or understand the need better. Put yourself in their situation and analyze the scenario. Would you like it if someone tried to sell you something that is of no use to you? You will try and avoid that company in the future as well because of your bad experience. Similarly, you must understand your customer base and their needs in order to sell the right product to the right person. This is where most people go wrong and end up upsetting people by trying to push their product to uninterested personnel.

One of the best techniques for closing could be to hear what the customer has to say. You should not talk all the time, by doing so you may miss out on certain key points which the customer has in their mind. And when you tend to listen to them, it builds a level of curiosity in them and you have a bright chance that will get inclined towards your sale. You need to ask something and then wait for him or her to finish completely. Some people have the habit of putting their thoughts in which will cause the customer to forget about the things that they had in mind. You need to be supportive and nod your head instead of trying to speak with them or for them.

Emotions play a crucial role in closing a sale. You need to check out the level of emotions the other person carries, while you are conversing with them. Try to always be on the positive side of their emotions which will allow you to close the sale in much effective manner. Again, nod your head and smile when they make an emotional point. Try and connect with them in such a way that they feel as though you relate to their problems or issues and are genuinely interested in helping them out. There needs to be a balance of emotional and logical actions when it comes to persuading a person to buy what you wish to sell to them. The two of you must develop a rapport which will help them trust you. Always put yourself in the customer's shoes to understand their needs and wants. If you pretend like you are clueless about what they are saying then they will be discouraged to speak out the truth. Similarly, if you say something contradicting to their thoughts just to sell your item then you will again end up discouraging them. All of it will ultimately result in the customer not interested in your product and might simply decide to play along.

And finally closing essentially doesn't mean the sale happened today. A multi-million dollar sale could take three years to complete and realize the value and money. So don't try and rush something and do your best to remain as positive as possible. If it is meant to happen then it will happen. You need not worry about it if you have done all the right things. It might take some time for the customer to be ready to shell out a lot of money but it will happen for sure if you have adopted all the right techniques to close your sale.

The most essential part is to maintain a relationship with your customer thinking long term and always try to find ways to close the deal effectively by using proven secrets and tips as mentioned in this book. Once you understand the various types of customers you come across and how to sell them, you have mastered the art of making them say 'yes' and make them say yes repeatedly. Once you garner confidence, you will be able to sell more and more of your product to many more customers and whether you are a salesman or a company dealing in the products, nobody will be able to stop you from making positive progress.

www.ingramcontent.com/pod-product-compliance
Lightning Source LLC
Chambersburg PA
CBHW070713250726
48662CB00001B/387